Poetry and Covid-19

POETRY and COVID-19

*An Anthology
of Contemporary International
and Collaborative Poetry*

Editors:
Anthony Caleshu & Rory Waterman

Shearsman Books

First published in the United Kingdom in 2021 by
Shearsman Books Ltd
PO Box 4239
Swindon
SN3 9FN

Shearsman Books Ltd Registered Office
30–31 St. James Place, Mangotsfield, Bristol BS16 9JB
(this address not for correspondence)

www.shearsman.com

ISBN 978-1-84861-759-9

This compilation copyright © Shearsman Books Ltd., 2021.

All rights in the Introduction and the poems printed here revert to their authors and translators after publication. Permissions requests may be directed to Shearsman Books, but they will be forwarded to the copyright-holders for decisions.

Acknowledgements

We gratefully acknowledge the UK Arts and Humanities Research Council, University of Plymouth, and Nottingham Trent University for their funded support of the Poetry & Covid project. Poetry & Covid also benefits from partnerships with various UK and international organisations including The Poetry Society, Poetry Wales, Poetry Ireland, Scottish Poetry Library, National Centre for Writing, and several UNESCO Cities of Literature: Heidelberg, Nottingham and Ulyanovsk. Lastly, we acknowledge here the work of our Research Assistant, Dr. Sam Kemp, who has not only helped in the production of this anthology, but tirelessly maintained the project website.

—AC and RW

CONTENTS

INTRODUCTION

'Pandemic Poetries', 7
Anthony Caleshu and Rory Waterman

POETRY COLLABORATIONS

Sinéad Morrissey and Jan Wagner (trans. Iain Galbraith) 33

Carol Leeming and Rakhshan Rizwan 43

George Szirtes and Alvin Pang 49

Vahni Capildeo and Vivek Narayanan 56

Rory Waterman and Togara Muzanenhamo 66

Rachael Allen and Ilya Kaminsky 71

Zoë Skoulding and Yana Lucila Lema Otavalo 79

Inua Ellams and Omar Musa 83

Matthew Welton and Hazel Smith 91

Vidyan Ravinthiran and Arvind Krishna Mehrotra 95

Anthony Caleshu and Mariko Nagai 103

Selima Hill and Wang Xiaoni (trans. Eleanor Goodman) 108

Declan Ryan and Linda Stern Zisquit 113

David Herd and Sharmistha Mohanty 118

Luke Kennard and Hwang Yu Won (trans. Jake Levine)	123
André Naffis-Sahely and Stacy Hardy	128
Harriet Tarlo and Craig Santos Perez	135
Jennifer Cooke and Jèssica Pujol Duran	139
Momtaza Mehri and A. E. Stallings	145
Contributors' Biographies	148

INTRODUCTION: PANDEMIC POETRIES

The publication of this anthology comes a year into the Covid-19 pandemic. In the summer of 2020, we invited nineteen UK poets to partner with poets from around the world, to work collaboratively on poems responding to the virus. The poems herein are as personal as they are communal, and as local as they are international. Between them, the writers reside in all of the world's permanently populated continents, recognising that the pandemic has truly hit us *everywhere*. Their diversities of aesthetics and poetics, of Covid experiences – at a distance and/or embodied, anecdotal and/or dramatic – are further significant to their inclusion and their work.

Below, we offer a short overview of pandemic poetries in English. It is, by necessity, both detailed and partial, objective and subjective. It concludes with mention of our ongoing Poetry and Covid project, of which this anthology plays one part in the documentation and artistic processing of our current crisis.

Anthony Caleshu and Rory Waterman

1.

'Like a cloud that travels on': from Bubonic Plague to Spanish Flu
(Rory Waterman)

It is October 2020, and I am in quarantine for fourteen days: the extra price I have to pay for a trip overseas as second waves of Covid-19 swell around the world. It is day six. I write this on the eleventh floor of The Splaisir Hotel in Myeongdong, Seoul, one of the busiest shopping districts on earth. This is one of many hotels within range of Incheon International Airport that is being used by the Korean government to quarantine new arrivals. Thankfully, the immovable desk where I write has been set by the room's little window, which I have discovered opens about six inches on one side with an unappealing suck. Below, the foundations are being laid for a new tower-block, and lilliputian figures move about in a muddle of mud and girders. My observations have taught me that it usually takes eight scoops from a Hyundai HX300 excavator to fill a lorry's dump trailer. Behind that organised chaos is the serene, squat headquarters of the Bank of Korea, pinned down at each corner by a shabby little green dome, and then a hundred tower-blocks, massive and ordinary, stretching out of sight in all directions – or all directions I can see within my ninety-degree radius on the world. Save for some signage and advertising hoardings using the Hangul alphabet, I could be anywhere that is, by some conceptions, somewhere. Cars and buses swing round the austere Bank of Korea fountain on the only bit of road I can see, but the little square beside it is eerily empty. A Chanel banner ruffles in the breeze, and huge LCDs screens pump out advertisements to tiny audiences – sometimes to no audiences at all. And yet, South Korea has become world famous for its ability to flatten the curve and keep it flat. Among developed nations, it is – at least for now – a 'success story'. And I think I have some personal experience of why. I am allowed to open the door to my room four times a day, to pick up breakfast, lunch and dinner from a plastic box or to drop my rubbish next to it, sprayed inside and out with disinfectant and tied in a heavy-duty orange binbag bearing a biohazard symbol. Security cameras in the corridor check I don't step across the threshold for any longer than is absolutely necessary, and daily announcements in seven languages remind me not to.

I am *not* complaining: this is a minor, if ultimately memorable, inconvenience. But it is also a reminder of how interconnected we have become. I am here to be a writer in residence for Bucheon UNESCO City of Literature, less than an hour away, but it so happens that I'll also get to spend time with an English friend I met as an undergraduate at the University of Leicester, who now lives in Incheon with his Chinese wife, and teaches at an American university there. That is three continents in one sentence, one chain of fairly quotidian facts. I came here in the conventional way: on a huge airliner, the product of thousands of minds, that no individual on earth could build, and fell asleep while travelling at five hundred miles an hour six miles above central Russia, Mongolia and China, and then diligently around North Korean airspace. It's all so extra-ordinary, all so completely normal.

You don't have to be an epidemiologist to understand how contagious diseases of zoonotic origin can arise apparently out of nowhere, develop into epidemics, and proliferate into pandemics in the increasingly crowded world so many of us – and so many of the systems within which we live – perpetuate. Four months after this virus was discovered in Wuhan at the end of 2019, New York City was filling 'morgue trucks' with bodies, and people across the UK were waving last goodbyes to parents through care home windows.[1] Nobody could yet even say for certain what the symptoms of Covid were, and no treatments had been developed – it had all happened so fast. But at least we have genuine hope of treatments being found – a more positive facet of the modernity that has brought all of these problems to us so quickly. It is probable that many of the epidemics and pandemics of the past might have followed a similarly rapid pattern of intercontinental transmission, had conditions allowed, though they still often made their way across and between continents eventually. And those caught up in earlier epidemics and pandemics had to contend with an 'invisible enemy' they had little means of coming to understand, to borrow the phraseology of a US President who has professed that he has 'the best words' at his disposal.

How has poetry – 'the best words in the best order', as Samuel Taylor Coleridge allegedly put it – regarded previous epidemics and pandemics?[2] The deadliest pandemic on record was the bubonic plague of 1348–53, which later came to be known as the Black Death. Between June 1348 and December 1350, it killed approximately half of the population of England; the next occurrence of bubonic plague in that country, in 1361, killed up to a fifth; and another, eight years later, was almost as deadly again. There were then successive waves of the plague at least once a decade for the next century, some lowering the population by as much as ten percent. This puts our current – and to us staggering – death tolls, and the duration of our privations, into perspective. It is surprising, then, that the Black Death, and successive waves of bubonic plague, do not have a more noticeable presence in late Medieval English poetry, especially considering that so many of the late medieval masters such as William Langland, the Gawain Poet and Geoffrey Chaucer lived through several of them. Chaucer might have taken Boccaccio's *The Decameron* as a

---

[1] Gina Cherelus, '"Dead Inside": The Morgue Trucks of New York City', *New York Times*, 27 May 2020 <https://www.nytimes.com/2020/05/27/opinion/coronavirus-morgue-trucks-nyc.html> [accessed 20 October 2020]; 'Coronavirus: Government sued Over Care Home Deaths "Disgrace"', BBC website, <https://www.bbc.co.uk/news/uk-england-devon-53012565> [accessed 20 October 2020].

[2] These words are attributed to Coleridge, but were written down by his nephew, Henry Nelson Coleridge, and first published posthumously in the latter's *Specimens of the Table Talk of the Late Samuel Taylor Coleridge* (1835).

model for *The Canterbury Tales*, but the most explicit reference to plague in his counterpart is in 'The Pardoner's Tale': 'a privee theef men clepeth [call] Deeth' who 'hath a thousand slayn this pestilence'.[3] Boccaccio's collection of novellas, by contrast, is a framed narrative in which what we might now call a 'bubble' of seven young women and three young men isolate from the Black Death in a villa outside Florence, and it contains gory depictions of what they left behind. In *Piers Plowman*, Langland went a little further that Chaucer in describing the effects of plague, 'with many kene sores, / As pokkes and pestilences' that 'kulled ful manye', but that seems to have been his longest explicit written mention of it.[4] A little later, John Lydgate (c.1370–1451) translated his 'Danse Macabre' 'owte of the frensshe' from a version in a Paris cemetery, and of course this also personifies 'cruel dethe', who is 'wyse and sage', and slays 'Bothe ȝonge [young] and olde' by 'stroke of pestilence'.[5] Lydgate is also responsible for 'Doctrine for Pestilence', a poem to be used as a guide or 'gouernance', for which reason it was immensely popular.[6] Attempted cures for plague at the time included such ingenious futilities as cutting a pigeon in two from the breast downwards and applying it, opened, to the patient's swellings before the bird died. For the most part, however, Lydgate's advice boils down to adjusting your diet to balance your humours: 'fro[m] frutes hold thyn abstinence' but eat 'chekenys' and 'Drynk good wyn'. It is wonderful, at least in retrospect, to think of poetry attempting to play this practical role in public health. But while poems can provide solace – we hope this anthology does that, among other things – any reader turning to poetry for medical advice now is probably looking in the wrong place.

Other expressly informative late medieval accounts of plague do exist, though none in English. One notable example is 'The Plague of Rhodes' (c. 1500) by Emmanuel Georgillas. There is no published full translation in English, though one might expect current scholarship to be clamouring to this task, considering the parallels.[7] Georgillas

---

[3] Geoffrey Chaucer, 'The Pardoner's Tale', in *The Riverside Chaucer*, ed. Larry D. Benson (3rd edn) (Oxford: Oxford University Press, 1988), p. 199.

[4] William Langland, *Piers the Plowman and Richard the Redeless*, ed. Walter W. Skeat (Oxford: Clarendon Press, 1886), p 584.

[5] Florence Warren, ed., *The Dance of Death: Edited from MSS. Ellesmere 26/A. 13 and B. M. Lansdowne 699* (Oxford: Oxford University Press, 1931), p. 24.

[6] Quoted in Bryon Lee Grigsby, *Pestilence in Medieval and Early Modern English Literature* (New York: Routledge, 2004), pp. 131–6.

7 I rely here on the partial translation provided in Costas Tsiamis et al, 'The

describes how 'The island of Rhodes was struck by God-sent death and suffering', and is apparently especially keen to forewarn 'you great rulers who lead us': 'listen to what this evil has been, this great and terrible shame'. Some of what he describes has chilling parallels with contemporary conditions in much of the world: he charts the mass burials outside town (to some extent comparable to the ones we saw on Hart Island near New York in the spring of 2020, for example),[8] how 'relatives and the neighbours' followed official orders to 'shut themselves into the houses' and the subsequent eeriness of the deserted streets, and the agony of personal suffering: 'I lost my wife and children / my three sisters and their husbands' and their children: 'the sword of Charon took them all'. In fact, by Georgillas's account, he lost twenty of his twenty-eight relatives, most of whom were children: unlike with Covid-19, young people were especially vulnerable to the Black Death. He also describes how it all began:

> a ship brought it when it moored in the harbour
> and on it Death was hiding in a sack
> and there the priest had gone to sell them eggs
> and Death sprang up and went to kiss him.

This is how medieval plagues spread across swathes of the globe: on trade routes. Like Covid-19, the Black Death likely originated in East Asia. It was a result of (albeit natural) climate change, which pushed infected rodents from depleted and drying marshes and grasslands towards urban areas. It then spread via the Silk Road to the Crimea, and from there – on fleas that were parasitic on rats aboard merchant ships – to North Africa, Western Asia and up through Europe. It arrived in England aboard a ship from the province of Gascony, the dispute over which had precipitated the Hundred Years' War. From there, it naturally made its way also into Scotland and Ireland. By the standards of the early twenty-first century, of course, that world of international trade and commerce seems extremely slow and primitive. Our civilisations, not least in the wasteful West, rely more than any other on globe-crossing transportation, in bulk and at

---

Knights Hospitaller of Rhodes and the Black Death of 1498', *Le Infezioni in Medicina* 3 (2018), pp. 283–94.

[8] 'New York Ramps Up Mass Burials Amid Outbreak', BBC website, 10 April 2020 <https://www.bbc.co.uk/news/world-us-canada-52241221> [accessed 20 October 2020].

speed; more of what we consume than ever comes from other places. And exponentially more of us travel internationally on a regular basis – or at least we did until the spring of 2020. Our medicine is, thankfully, greatly improved; but modern pestilences can emerge and spread like never before, and of course they are doing. Something needs to be done. Nobody quite knows what, without the sort of compromises that neither many of us, nor the governments and corporate interests that rule so much of our lives, can contemplate.

The plague's demographic effects also often had something in common with modern realities. For example, it affected urban areas more than rural ones, and the poor more than the rich, primarily because the poor had less access to nursing, typically lived in closer proximity to one another, and did not have the means to flee to the countryside and winter it out. It also precipitated uprisings – perhaps most notably, in England, the Peasant's Revolt of 1381, a consequence of resentments between serfs and landowners after labourers' wages had increased following a huge drop in the population. This initiated a huge social change: the eventual abolition of serfdom in England. It is undoubtedly the case, then, that the plagues of the Middle Ages sped up an inevitable, if grindingly slow, move towards equality, with transformative effects on all facets of life, including poetry. It just didn't leave much of a direct mark on the art in English at the time. Covid-19, by comparison – and as we shall see in the second section of this introduction – has already been written about in poems a great deal, though how much of that work will endure is a matter for time, the great sifter, to determine.

From the late fifteenth century onwards, outbreaks of bubonic plague in the British Isles tended to be localised. Nonetheless, it recurred at reasonably frequent intervals until well into the eighteenth century, occasionally killing up to a quarter of the populations in the cities and towns it afflicted. Several of the Renaissance dramatists clearly demonstrate an awareness that contagion is not only airborne, but transmitted by expiration: in John Webster's *The White Devil*, 'your breath: / Out upon sweetmeats and continued physic – / The plague is in them',[9] and in Shakespeare's *King John*, Melun refers to 'black contagious breath',[10]

---

[9] John Webster, *The White Devil*, ed. Christina Luckyj (London: Bloomsbury, 2014), p. 36.

[10] William Shakespeare, *The Oxford Shakespeare: The Complete Works*, ed. John Jowett, William Montgomery, Gary Taylor, and Stanley Wells (Oxford: Clarendon Press, 1986), p. 448.

among many examples. The most common explanation for the origin of the contagion, of course, was divine intervention. Nevertheless, some things had been learned, and methods of containment had improved significantly, many of them not dissimilar to the ones we see today: 'Bills of Mortality' gave regular death figures, parish by parish; ships were held in harbour until it could be confirmed there were no cases on board; the sick faced quarantine and watchmen ensured they observed it. Even my current, extremely comfortable counterpart to that experience seems memorable enough to write about – but how to do it, with more than just passing reference? Shakespeare didn't, though it is well known that he turned to writing sonnets as a means of earning income when plague shut London's theatres – his own ingenious furlough retention scheme, if you will. Shakespeare's fellow playwright Thomas Dekker turned to pamphleteering in the 1603 epidemic, publishing *The Wonderfull Yeare*, in which he proclaimed that one could 'fill a hundred paire of writing tables with notes' after witnessing 'one hour on this stage',[11] but few of his contemporaries converted any of their notes into poems. One exception was Ben Jonson, whose elegy 'On my first Son' does not mention the plague directly, only that his child had escaped the 'world's and flesh's rage, / And if no other misery, yet age'.[12]

However, plague returns as metaphor or point of comparison in a huge number of poems. In John Donne's 'Love's Deity', insincere love is a 'deeper plague'.[13] The events in Jonathan Swift's satire 'The Beasts' Confession' occur 'when a plague broke out / (Which there-fore made them more devout)'.[14] Alfred Lord Tennyson's 'Demeter and Persephone' speaks of 'younger, kindlier' Gods who 'quench, not hurl the thunderbolt' and 'stay, / Not spread the plague'.[15] Samuel Taylor Coleridge's 'Fears in Solitude' sets a love of Britain where he has 'drunk in' all his 'ennobling thoughts' against the influence of the nation overseas:

---

[11] Thomas Dekker, *The Plague Pamphlets*, ed. F. P. Wilson (Oxford: Oxford University Press, 1923), p. 21.

[12] Ben Jonson, *The Complete Poems*, ed. George Parfitt (London: Penguin, 1975), p. 48.

[13] John Donne, *Selected Poems*, ed. Ilona Bell (London: Penguin, 2006), p. 41.

[14] Jonathan Swift, *The Works of Dr. Jonathan Swift*, vol. 7 (London: W. Bowyer, 1768), p. 360

[15] Alfred, Lord Tennyson, *The Complete Works* (New York: Frederick A. Stokes, 1891), p. 433.

> Like a cloud that travels on,
> Steamed up from Cairo's swamps of pestilence,
> Even so, my countrymen! have we gone forth
> And borne to distant tribes slavery and pangs,
> And, deadlier far, our vices [...].[16]

Particularly prescient, given recent conversations about the legacy of slavery in the United States, is the black American twentieth-century poet Robert Hayden's historical poem 'Middle Passage', which describes among many privations onboard slave ships 'A plague among / our blacks – ophthalmia: blindness'.[17]

Of course, almost every epidemic on record has been documented in poetry to some extent. Most frequently mentioned among these is probably syphilis, 'the Great Pox', partly because of the licentiousness with which it is often associated – and not only in the common interjection 'a pox on' whatever has raised the speaker's heckles in countless works of Renaissance drama. However, again, few poets wrote about it in detail, though in his poem 'To the Quene' the late medieval Scottish poet William Dunbar describes how syphilis makes men feeble 'lyk willing wandis [wands]', and suggests a preventative measure: 'Keip fra harlottis nycht and day'.[18] The earliest known work in English-language poetry about smallpox, which afflicted Britain from the late sixteenth century onwards, is Thomas Spillman's 'Upon His Ladies Sickenesse of the Smalle Pockes' (1602): 'Cruel and unpartiall Sicknesse, / Sword of that Arch-Monarke Death, / That subdues all strength by weaknesse'. His lady has survived, but he can 'tracke' the marks of the illness 'In the pure snow of thy face'.[19] Half a century later, John Dryden was compelled to write his elegy 'Upon the Death of Lord Hastings'. This is certainly not his finest verse. Indeed, it is almost ludicrous. But, like Spillman, Dryden also draws attention to the physical impacts of the disease – and lingers on them:

---

[16] Samuel Taylor Coleridge, *The Poetical Works* (London: Frederick Warne, 1892), p. 139.

[17] Robert Hayden, *The Collected Poems*, ed. Frederick Glaysher (New York: Norton, 2013), p. 48.

[18] William Dunbar, *The Poems*, ed. David Laing (Edinburgh: Laing and Fobes, 1834), p. 116.

[19] Thomas Spillman, *A Poetical Rhapsody*, ed. H. E. Rollins (Cambridge, MA: Harvard University Press, 1931), p. 222.

> Blisters with pride swelled, which through 's flesh did sprout
> Like rosebuds, stuck i' the lily-skin about.
> Each little Pimple had a Tear in it,
> To wail the fault its rising did commit. [...]
> No comet need foretell his change drew on,
> Whose corpse might seem a constellation.[20]

From the early nineteenth century onwards, there are quite a few poems in English about cholera, though many of these have an attendant focus on poverty, which implies poets were often seeing that pandemic as a vehicle for discussion of wider social conditions. In *Chaunt of the Cholera: Songs for Ireland*, John and Michael Banim personify cholera as a mercenary: 'Kings! tell me my commission, / As from land to land I go'.[21] In 'The Garden by the Bridge', Violet Nicolson (who wrote under the pseudonym Laurence Hope) evokes 'Poor beasts, and poorer men': 'Parias steal the rotten railway sleeper / To burn the bodies of their cholera dead'.[22] And Rudyard Kipling's several evocations of the virus include the soldiers' ballad 'Cholera Camp', which describes how the disease is 'before us, an' be'ind us, an' we cannot get away, / An' the doctor's just reported we've ten more to-day': the job of these low-ranking, working-class men is to keep on going in spite of the dangers.[23]

War and disease are often closely connected in the public conscience, and in literature – and not only because war often spreads disease. 'Spanish Flu' was so named because the press in neutral Spain was not subjected to censorship during the Great War of 1914–18, and was free to report on the illness, giving the false impression the country was especially badly hit. In fact, it probably originated in a Kansas army camp, and came to the trenches with American soldiers in 1918. From there, it spread from Russia across Asia, and into Africa. Armistice celebrations in Allied nations then proved perfect breeding grounds. The downsides to modernisation were felt keenly, both in terms of

---

[20] John Dryden, *The Works*, ed. Sir Walter Scott and George Saintsbury (Edinburgh: William Paterson, 1885), p. 96.

[21] John Banim and Michael Banim, *Chaunt of the Cholera and Songs for Ireland* (London: James Cochrane, 1831), p. 6.

[22] Laurence Hope, *India's Love Lyrics* (Garden City, NY: Garden City Publishing, 1901), p. 56.

[23] Rudyard Kipling, *Barrack-Room Ballads and Other Verses 1885–1891* (Teddington: Echo, 2004), pp. 193–4.

the mechanisation and chemicalisation of battle, and the ready global transmission of contagion. That pandemic infected up to a third of the world's population and claimed considerably more lives than the Great War (estimates put the figure at fifty to one hundred million) in half the time, but again brought us very little notable poetry, even though many poets were nearly killed by it, including H. D., D. H. Lawrence and T. S. Eliot. This had most certainly not been true of the first global, mechanised war: 'man's inhumanity to man' at its most brutal was bound to inspire poets to ask questions a pandemic could not raise. The Spanish Flu was subsequently pushed to the back of the collective memory and almost forgotten for a century, but it does undoubtedly play a significant if often subtle role in much of the literature of the period, and this is often overlooked. As Elizabeth Outka has pointed out, 'When we fail to read for illness in general, and the 1918 pandemic in particular, we reify how military conflict has come to define history. […] If we know what to look out for, the literature of the era emerges as particularly adept at representing the pandemic's particular qualities and its vast yet hidden presence'.[24] Outka makes a compelling case that we might read works such as Eliot's *The Waste Land* and Yeats's 'The Second Coming' through this lens, even though neither addresses the matter explicitly. The latter is very obviously concerned with political flux in Ireland and the after-effects of global war, but are we missing something if we read it only in this light? After all, the pandemic affected almost everybody, and our distance from it now should not blind us to the fact that it was a viral horror unique in the lifetimes of almost everybody, and pervaded people's daily experiences at least as much as the current pandemic pervades ours. Yeats wrote the poem weeks after his pregnant wife had nearly died from the virus, which gives a secondary resonance to the poem's claim 'That twenty centuries of stony sleep / Were vexed to nightmare by a rocking cradle'.[25] 'Mere anarchy is loosed upon the world', writes Yeats in the first stanza, and today, perhaps more than ever, we can hear in Yeats' 'mere' the incongruity of the great devastation that might be wreaked from something as tiny as a virion.

---

[24] Elizabeth Outka, *Viral Modernism: The Influenza Pandemic and Interwar Literature* (New York: Columbia University Press, 2019), p. 2.

[25] W. B. Yeats, *Selected Poems*, ed. Timothy Webb (London: Penguin, 2000), p. 124.

2.
'Vexed' and 'Humming', Metaphors and Impurities: from HIV/AIDS to Covid-19
(Anthony Caleshu)

'If I can't leave you / Dead, I'll have / You vexed', writes Jericho Brown in his persona poem, 'The Virus', from his Pulitzer Prize winning collection, *The Tradition*, published in 2019. The poem might now seem like a prophecy but, as Brown notes in interview, 'in many ways that poem is thinking about HIV's history.'[26] In using the definite article in his title, Brown highlights the status of HIV as 'The' virus which has (at least until Covid-19) most disrupted our contemporary world order, a virus which has invidiously 'vexed' us (echoing Yeats' 'The Second Coming'). Brown metaphorically connects this vexing to what we take to be historical griefs – over a world that discriminates on the basis of sexuality, gender, class, race etc., unnamed in the poem, but perhaps implicitly inciting the 'anger' of those who study American history:

> I want you
> To heed that I'm still here
> Just beneath your skin and in
> Each organ
> The way anger dwells in a man
> Who studies the history of his nation.

In the late twentieth and early twenty-first century, there have been several viruses which have reached pandemic levels, but it wasn't until HIV/AIDS that poets began to respond *en masse*. Before Covid-19, SARS (severe acute respiratory syndrome) and MERS (Middle East respiratory syndrome), were the two most well-known *coronaviruses* (outside of those responsible for the common cold), with major outbreaks from 2002 and 2012 respectively and recording upwards of 1000 deaths each.[27] 'Swine' flu of 2009–2010 was responsible for hundreds of

---

[26] Jericho Brown, in Conversation with Michael Dumanis, *Bennington Review*, 27 October 2018, https://www.benningtonreview.org/jericho-brown-interview [accessed 12 January 2021]

[27] Elisabeth Mahase, 'Coronavirus: covid-19 has killed more people than SARS and MERS combined, despite lower case fatality rate', BMJ (18 February 2020) <https://www.bmj.com/content/368/bmj.m641> [accessed 2

thousands of deaths world-wide,[28] but it, like the others, received very few poetic responses, perhaps no more than the perennial poems that emerge about run-of-the-mill flus the world over every year.[29] Though a single death of anyone at any one time can spur a million poems and more readers, poetic responses, it seems, at the larger scale I'm interested in here, come with global reach, with millions of infections and deaths, not to mention a revolution in world-order, requiring a total revamp of how we think about and live our daily lives.

And so to HIV – the human immunodeficiency virus – and its late-stage disease AIDS – acquired immunodeficiency syndrome. I spell these out now to slow down my own use of these acronyms which, as acronyms will, in their shorthandedness, have a way of being passed over, glossed, rendered blasé. In his 2014 essay, 'In Time of Plague', John McIntyre explores 'how poetry about AIDS has shifted through the years,'[30] nodding to the many writers who have now become staples in discussions of its place in poetry: Tim Dlugos, Reginald Shepherd, Joel Zizik, Henri Cole, Paul Monette, Eileen Myles, Rafael Campo, Thom Gunn, Mark Doty, D. A. Powell, as well as the younger generation of poets including Saeed Jones and the aforementioned Jericho Brown. Since the virus hit in the 1980s, it is estimated that over 75 million people have become infected with HIV and over 30 million have died from AIDS-related illnesses world-wide.[31] Countless poems, collections, and anthologies have been published, attesting to poetry as a mode of discourse to document and explore how the virus has affected the human condition. Thomas Lux's review of Rachel Hadas's 1991 anthology *Unending Dialogue: Voices from an AIDS Poetry Workshop* concludes with reference to the importance of poetic response in the face of the callous *laissez faire* attitude that dominated American politics in the 1980s: 'Would this book never had to be written. Would that it gets nailed to

---

January 2021].

[28] See '2009, H1N1 Pandemic', Centre for Disease Control, <https://www.cdc.gov/flu/pandemic-resources/2009-h1n1-pandemic.html> [accessed 12 January 2021].

[29] For an excellent poem that responds to swine flu, see Robyn Schiff, 'H1N1'

[30] John McIntyre, 'In Time of Plague', https://www.poetryfoundation.org/articles/70183/in-time-of-plague [accessed 2 January 2021]

[31] 'Global HIV & AIDS statistics – 2020 fact sheet', UNAIDS <https://www.unaids.org/en/resources/fact-sheet> [accessed 2 January 2021].

the White House door.'³² The best poetry produced over the years bears the Lux-like sense of necessity – the need for art to intervene where other measures fail (political, economic, medical, and any variety of socio-cultural measures). As MacIntyre nears the end of his essay, he makes reference to Sarah Schulman, who rightly reminds us:

> We still have to work every day to assert the obvious, that in fact, there are two distinctly different kinds of AIDS that are not over.
> 1. There is AIDS of the past.
> 2. There is ongoing AIDS.³³

Almost 40 years after the first diagnosed death from AIDS-related complications in 1981, and now, today, with a battery of anti-virals in place but still no vaccine in sight, the disease continues to draw the attention of the arts, not least of all poetry. Perhaps, in part, this is due to what Reginald Shepherd highlights in his essay, 'Illness and Poetry', as 'there [being] something both poetic and reproachful to poetry in HIV's literalization, its materialization, of the sex/death nexus so common as a poetic trope.'³⁴ Alternative reasons for the arts' place in the ongoing legacy of the virus are presented by Schulman, who argues that the arts (radical, as they need be) can challenge the white-washed 'gentrification' of the disease and its infection of us physically, spiritually, and imaginatively: the physical gentrification of AIDS is marked by 'the removal of communities of diverse classes, ethnicities, races, sexualities, languages, and points of view […] by more homogenized groups'; its 'spiritual' gentrification 'affect[s] people who did not have rights, who were not represented, who did not have power or even consciousness about their reality of their own condition'; and finally the virus's 'gentrification of

---

³² Thomas Lux, *Harvard Review* 1 (1992), pp. 192–193. <www.jstor.org/stable/27559461> [accessed 2 January 2021].

³³ Cited in McIntyre, Sarah Schulman, *The Gentrification of the Mind* (Berkeley, CA: University of California Press, 2012).

³⁴ Reginald Shepherd, 'Illness and Poetry,' Poetry Foundation website (8 March 2008) <https://www.poetryfoundation.org/harriet/2008/03/illness-and-poetry> [accessed 8 January 2021]. Considering this, how apt that one of the multi-systemic disorder syndromes that can manifest in those with HIV goes by the acronym POEMS (polyneuropathy, organomegaly, endocrinopathy, M protein, skin changes).

the mind [represents] an internal replacement that alienated people from the concrete process of social and artistic change.'[35]

What can be done about this? How can we combat the virus with the arts, when the promise of 'artistic change', itself, is compromised by the virus? Both the old and a new generation of writers continue to champion that change can come, an attempt to rewrite the future and to push it beyond the reaches of the past.[36] And yet, if we want to manage our contemporary human condition with dignity (at the biological, social, economic, political and cultural levels), we know we need to acknowledge the past, even when a virus seems utterly novel.

'"Plague" is the principal metaphor by which the AIDS epidemic is understood', Susan Sontag writes in *AIDS and its Metaphors*, elaborating:

> AIDS is understood in a premodern way, as a disease incurred by people both as individuals and as members of a "risk group" – that neutral-sounding, bureaucratic, category which also revives the archaic idea of a tainted community that illness has judged.[37]

The 1980s response to HIV/AIDS was not unlike the fourteenth-century response to the bubonic plague, by which I mean, in general, people were quicker to judge than to help. America was guilty of this in extremis and, after the first cases were reported, the Reagan administration did so little for so long that it resulted in decades of unnecessary death due to ignorance, intolerance, and fear of gay life and sexuality. 'Plagues are invariably regarded as judgments on society [...] punishments not just of individuals but of a group', Sontag writes.[38] And yet, at the same time, the artistic response was unlike any seen before, with writers quick to challenge the prevailing narrative, several going on to win national and international recognition, becoming voices of not only HIV/AIDS, but of their generation – this includes a good few of those poets already cited. These writers tackle the subject of

---

[35] Schulman, p. 14.

[36] See projects such as *HIV Here & Now* and their 'one-year countdown in poems to 35 years of AIDS on June 5, 2016' <https://www.hivhereandnow.com/> [accessed 2 January 2021].

[37] Susan Sontag, *Illness as Metphor, and Aids and Its Metaphors* (London: Penguin, 1991): pp. 130, 132.

[38] Sontag, 140.

the virus (and often their experience with the virus) in individual ways, both via personal anecdote and philosophical inquiry, blurring the lines between the literal/explicit and the implicit/metaphoric (consider *The Man with Night Sweats*, as Thom Gunn titled one of his books, or the tell-tale symptom of 'Kaposi's sarcoma', described by Reginald Shepherd as 'harsh syllables pronounced / across the skin, the purple lesions almost / hyacinth'[39]), in both cases giving what might have been an abstracted subject tangibility so to connect it to a wider readership.

Despite such direct treatment, one thing many of the writers had in common was an unwillingness to be read *only* as HIV/AIDS poets. D. A. Powell, for instance, in his introduction to his first book of poetry, *Tea* (1998), refuses to give the disease full congress as subject. He begins the introduction: 'This is not a book about AIDS. […] I do not deny this disease its impact. But I deny its dominion.'[40] Interestingly, though Sontag argues for the prevalence of 'AIDS as a metaphor for contamination and mutation',[41] Powell denies metaphor as impetus for writing about the virus:

> While I was writing these poems, a well-known poet, who is also queer, cautioned me against using AIDS as a metaphor for a consumptive relationship. I do not understand "metaphor." I have the sort of mind that lumps together odd events, that enjoys the simultaneity of experience… If two objects occupy the same space is one a metaphor for the other? If so then life is the cause of death; love, the root of unhappiness.[42]

Powell goes on to contemplate 'failed love, destitution, prostitution, disease, homelessness, and myriad other subjects in order to discover that the true hero of the poems is survival'.[43] And it is *survival*, of course, that is exactly at stake – perhaps, in some strange mode of inversion, it might even be becoming a metaphor for AIDS, itself? Consider the poet Tory Dent who, for so long and so well, wrote of surviving AIDS-

---

[39] Reginald Shepherd, 'Kindertotenlieder', *Some Are Drowning* (Pittsburgh, PA: University of Pittsburgh Press, 1995).

[40] D. A. Powell. *Tea* (Middletown, CT: Wesleyan University Press, 1998), p. xi.

[41] Sontag, p. 153.

[42] Powell, p. xii.

[43] Powell, pp. xii-xiii.

related complications until finally succumbing in 2005, and of whom Stanley Kunitz, the US Poet Laureate at the time, wrote: 'Tory's language uncoils with such vitality, it would seem that speaking were an act of the immune system, a primary means of survival.'[44] Is it this literal and, likewise, metaphorical drive to survive that unites all pandemic poetries? Powell's push into the territory of survival makes punning reference to the biology of the matter, conflating (I'd argue metaphorically, again, despite himself) prison work with what it means to die of the disease:

> gary asleep in his recliner.   this prison work clobbers him.
>   today let the men stand unguarded
> he is overwhelmed by his own cells   a furtive shiv behind his
>   eyes [...][45]

At other times, he writes head-on of the ironies and indignities of a disease which conflates the somatic space of sex and death – again, a directness which verges on the metaphorical in its rhetorical (and projective) versifying: 'leaking from the socket of his anus: coytus.   he stands apart involuntary.   pooped himself'.[46] For sure, this is a poetry of 'moments both pure and impure', as he writes in a later poem.[47]

One of the defining tenets of twentieth- and twenty-first-century poetry is expressed by Pablo Neruda, in his short essay 'Towards an Impure Poetry', where he praises '[t]he used surfaces of things, the wear that the hands give to things, the air, tragic at times, pathetic at others, of such things.' He steers us to the tangible – 'the mandates of touch, smell, taste, sight, hearing' – to recognise that 'all lend a curious attractiveness to the reality of the world that should not be underprized.'[48]

---

[44] Wolfgang Saxon, 'Tory Dent, Poet Who Wrote of Living with HIV Dies at 47', *New York Times* (3 January 2006) <https://www.nytimes.com/2006/01/03/arts/tory-dent-poet-who-wrote-of-living-with-hiv-dies-at-47.html> [accessed 2 January 2021]. See any number of Dent poems for what it means to live with treatment of the disease, including 'R.I.P., My Love': 'translucent infrastructure of IVs / and oxygen tubes superimposed itself upon me / like a body double, more virulent and cold, like / Leda pinned and broken by her swan', from *HIV, Mon Amour* (Riverdale-on-Hudson, NY: Sheep Meadow Press, 1999).

[45] Powell, p. 4.

[46] Powell, p. 6.

[47] Powell, p. 8.

[48] Pablo Neruda. *Five Decades: Poems 1925–1970*, trans. B. Belitt (New York,

As a characteristic of the avant-garde movement, 'Impure Poetry' is 'an attempt to reintegrate art into social praxis', Rafik Al Massoudi tells us.[49] To write of HIV/AIDS is not to write merely of its extremes, its dramas of illness and death – but to be socially-engaged, to write of the social praxis constituted by the everyday, in a language which is as domestic as it is dutiful.

I was studying for my MFA at the University of Alabama in 1995 when Mark Doty came to Tuscaloosa and gave a reading in the old-world lecture hall, enormous plush red velvet curtains hanging heavy behind him as he read his long eponymous poem 'Atlantis', about his partner Wally, who had died of AIDS-related complications the year before:

> I swear sometimes
> when I put my head to his chest
> I can hear the virus humming
>
> like a refrigerator.
> Which is what makes me think
> you can take your positive attitude
>
> and go straight to hell.
> We don't have a future,
> we have a dog.[50]

In these lines, Doty domesticates the virus – in the appliance of a refrigerator, in the pet of a dog – eventually in the language of the doctor, who 'wrote / not even a real word / but an acronym, a vacant / four-letter cipher // that draws meanings into itself, reconstitutes the world.' By virtue of this domestication, Doty introduces the virus into the reality of Western, first-world lives, invoking a manner which is as common as it is socio-politically engaged; because, regardless of our sexuality, or whether one has the virus or not, we (almost all of us) have refrigerators, have (or know those who have) dogs.

Doty, like Powell and the other poets mentioned, is aligned with Neruda's 'impurity' in 'the sumptuous appeal of the tactile.' Part of that

---

NY: Grove Press, 1974), p. xxi.

[49] Rafik Al Massoudi, 'The "Impure" Identity in Neruda's Poetry: Plural Identities', *The International Journal of Literary Humanities* 13.2 (2015), pp. 9–15.

[50] Mark Doty, *Atlantis* (New York: Harper Perennial, 1995), p. 50.

tactility is of the very language which haunts us, not just at the point of diagnosis, but for the ongoing commitment to how it comes to define us:

> We tried to say it was just
>
> a word; we tried to admit
> it had power and thus to nullify it
> by means of our acknowledgement.[51]

Doty's remembrance of 'your illness a kind of solvent / dissolving the future a little at a time'[52] is all the more poignant for its methodical progression through anecdotes about dreams and friends and our human desire to comfort (and to be comforted) when nothing – not even language – will comfort. And yet, writing about *Fire to Fire: New and Selected Poems* (2008), Reginald Shepherd is right to conclude his review with an allusion to Doty's own meta-ambition: 'The poems combine close attention to the fragile, contingent things of the world with the constant, almost unavoidable chance of transcendence, since "desire can make anything into a god."'[53]

How can we write our way out of a pandemic – or, rather, into a space where we begin to process abstract feelings of loneliness, illness, unhappiness, financial woe, grief, anxiety, general malaise or melancholy? Neruda concludes his essay:

> Melancholy, old mawkishness impure and unflawed, fruits of a fabulous species lost to the memory, cast away in a frenzy's abandonment – moonlight, the swan in the gathering darkness, all hackneyed endearments: surely that is the poet's concern, essential and absolute.
>
> Those who shun the 'bad taste' of things will fall flat on the ice.[54]

---

[51] Doty, p. 50.

[52] Doty, p. 57.

[53] Reginald Shepherd, review of Mark Doty, *Fire to Fire: New and Selected Poems*, *Publisher's Weekly* <https://www.publishersweekly.com/978-0-06-075247-7> [accessed 8, January 2021].

[54] Neruda, p. xxi.

I've puzzled over these lines for years. Does Neruda want us to pursue the mawkish, the bad taste of a hackneyed literature? No. He just wants us *not* to fear the sentiments of such, to pursue those *ur-feelings* which are true in their absoluteness and which we take for granted as human. There are no new feelings, just new expressions of old hats, old worries and melancholies, happinesses and wonders; we'll forever be lost and found, living and dying. The viruses that have so adversely affected our world for thousands of years are, at their base level, levellers of our collective feelings. In his metaphoric instruction to write an 'impure' poetry, Neruda, like Shepherd after him, correlates poetry with a viral-like ability to contaminate the 'surface of things, the tragic air' – a communicable, gross reminder of our fragility and our need for medical, social, economic, and cultural intervention. In other words, the very viruses which destroy our human condition are worthy of a poetry which preserves it, which can help us to capture how we're 'vexed' (to use Jericho Brown's word), which can help us weather the banality of domestic duties, job losses, social lockdowns, Zooming, premature illness, even the extremes of death. Such a poetry both reaches low into the depths of our recessed thoughts and action about what it means to live in the midst of a pandemic, and rises up to certain dizzying heights, allowing us to approach meaning and feeling.

I'm writing this at the end of 2020, a year into the Covid-19 pandemic. There have been over 1.8 million deaths due to the virus, and over 83 million infections (the global rate of which is starting to rise again).[55] Even if one has been lucky enough not to have first-hand experience of the virus, no one on our planet has been removed from its adverse effects on our usual ways of life. Though Covid-19 is, for most, an acute disease (as opposed to the chronic nature of HIV/AIDS), our current pandemic, like those before it, has been marked by outbreaks followed closely by public anxiety (both panic and denial), government inattention (and likewise assurances that all will be just fine), and perhaps most honestly, clinical confusion about how to respond. This isn't to chastise the authorities' responses (that's the subject of a different essay), so much as simply to refer to the fact that during times of such crisis, it is hard to know what to do, how to live, how to 'survive'.

From the beginning of the Covid-19 crisis, almost surprisingly for such a marginal art (outside the limelight at the best of times), poetry

---

[55] 'Our World In Data' <https://ourworldindata.org/covid-deaths#what-is-the-total-number-of-confirmed-deaths> [accessed 31 December 2020].

has offered solace if not solutions, valued by politicians, medics, and the general public alike as a way to comprehend and situate ourselves.[56] It has enabled us to reintegrate, reconnect, rethink and rearticulate our humanity in a time when division is being fostered by lockdown(s), now in successive waves. In the first months of Covid-19, a poem beginning 'And the people stayed home', went (fittingly) viral on social media, frequently alongside the claim that it had been written in 1869 and 're-printed during the 1919 pandemic'.[57] In fact, it had been written in March 2020, just as the West was going into its first lockdowns, by a retired teacher from Wisconsin, Kitty O'Meara, who told of writing it in 20 minutes, about what she was seeing right in front of her, and published it on her Facebook blog. If nothing else, this proved that, in one fundamental way, at least, our experiences had commonality with those of the past. Pandemics may require distancing, both physical and social. They may force us into emotional and spiritual distance from our very selves, but they also require future hopes. In April, the *Wall Street Journal* published an expose on 'Pandemic Poetries', the author noting the value of the art during such extreme times of duress;[58] similarly the *Japan Times* began to publish readers' poems about the pandemic (as did newspapers around the world); and, in the thick of the first lockdown, Ireland's Taoiseach, Leo Varadkar, quoted Nobel Laureate Seamus Heaney (albeit not one of his poems): 'If we winter this one out. We can summer anywhere'.[59]

---

[56] For an excellent exploration of how historical plagues have been represented within and beyond literature see Jennifer Cooke, *Legacies of Plague in Literature, Theory and Film* (London: Palgrave Macmillan, 2009).

[57] Nora Krug, 'The Story behind 'And the People Stayed Home,' the little poem that became so much more', *Washington Post* (10 December 2020) <https://www.washingtonpost.com/entertainment/books/and-the-people-stayed-home-poem/2020/12/09/3f2411fe-3961-11eb-bc68-96af0daae728_story.html> [accessed 8 January 2021].

[58] 'Gregg Opelka, 'Poetry for a Pandemic', *Wall Street Journal* (6 April 2020) <https://www.wsj.com/articles/poetry-for-a-pandemic-11586214366> [accessed 8 January 2020]. Also see 'Poems from a Pandemic: Three Poets Reflect on life in the age of Covid-19', *Wall Street Journal* (4 June 2020) <https://www.wsj.com/articles/poems-from-a-pandemic-11591294568> [accessed 8 January 2021].

[59] See <https://www.seamusheaney.com/news-and-events/2020/4/10/if-we-winter-this-one-out-we-can-summer-anywhere> [accessed 8 January 2021].

The idea that poetry might help us to survive this pandemic is the subject of our ongoing *Poetry and Covid* project – a project which runs with thanks to the support of the universities where we work as academics, the University of Plymouth and Nottingham Trent University, as well as the UK Arts and Humanities Research Council. In June 2020, at the time when we were commissioning the poetry collaborations in this book, we created the *poetryandcovid.com* website, which invites public submissions. In our efforts to collect and communicate a wide breadth of poetic responses and to document a diversity of experiences, the website's tale, almost ironically, is of a shared pandemic. Instead of repetition and 'sameness', however, we are finding that poetry, in its very differences, has begun to take the shape of the necessary 'collective thinking, reasoning, and imagination to create a healthier world' (as *Boston Review* called for art to do early in the pandemic's first spring of 2020),[60] and to facilitate the World Health Organisation's recognized need for people worldwide to respond with 'solidarity'.[61] It has long been intrinsically understood that there is therapeutic value in reading and writing poetry,[62] a stance the website maintains with each new day's submissions and publications, attesting to how poetry can aid our personal and cultural health and wellbeing, confirming our project's aims to speak to our human quest to, if not always understand, at least give voice to our predicaments.

Through the end of 2020, the website has had over 50,000 views, publishing almost 300 poets and 500 poems responding to the pandemic, as well as facilitating 'connections' between the site's readers and writers both, including hundreds of written comments which have likewise extended the reach of poetry via social media posts, likes, and tweets – certainly not new methods of exchange in our 21st century, but increasingly relied on to communicate life in our nearly ubiquitously locked-down world. We are heartened by how poetry has served writers and readers alike – poems of grief, anger, loneliness, communion, wonder,

---

[60] *Boston Review*, March 27, 2020, http://bostonreview.net/science-nature/thinking-pandemic [accessed, 10 May 2020]

[61] See <https://www.who.int/news/item/03-04-2020-who-and-unicef-to-partner-on-pandemic-response-through-covid-19-solidarity-response-fund> [accessed 10 May 2020]

[62] See, for example, 'Centre for Research into Reading, Literature and Society', University of Liverpool e thinking, reasoning, and imagination to <https://www.liverpool.ac.uk/humanities-social-sciences-health-medicine-technology/reading-literature-and-society/> [accessed 8 January 2021].

hope, political angst, and, not incidentally, humour. It is not uncommon to read comments referring to the 'poignancy of these poems' that 'capture our collective experience', occasionally to attest to 'saving my life.'[63] At the point of conception, our project set out to be and remains for all those directly and indirectly affected by the crisis, including the infirm, the vulnerable, the elderly, school-children, the bereaved, the lonely, not to mention any and all needing a jolt of imaginative rejuvenation and solace. Poetry, so we believe, is a useful form of discourse to combat the adverse ramifications of the virus, helping people better to deal with common mental health symptoms, grief, and the 'dearth of inspiration' suffered due to social distancing, as researchers noted in a coronavirus edition of *National Geographic* published in the Spring of 2020.[64] Not incidentally, the website's daily updates of submissions and publications, has also enabled us to follow the machinations of the pandemic as it spreads, documenting and reflecting on applicable health, economic, social, cultural, scientific and political concerns. In this way, the website and this anthology, both, constitute interdisciplinary resources, whereby poetry meets the physical and social sciences, as well as the health sector. As a whole, the project hopes to provide a unique legacy regarding poetic responses to Covid-19, fulfilling our role as publishers and editors to act as 'guardians of historical memory'.[65]

Whilst we invite readers to visit the website (and to contribute their own poems), we end this preface as we began it, with acknowledgement to this anthology you hold in your hands. As editors, we commissioned 19 pairs of poets to respond to Covid-19, with the intention to investigate how poetry might serve as a mode of discourse to explore the pandemic. Though poems are generally made alone, the task we asked our contributors to accept was to write collaboratively. We believe this anthology's emphasis on collaboration offers a novel way to address a

---

[63] See comments to the poetry of Laura Grace Weldon, whose poems were published on 17 September 2020, and which have been shared upwards of 300 times [accessed 10 January, 2021]. <https://poetryandcovid.com/2020/09/17/three-poems-9/>.

[64] *National Geographic*, https://www.nationalgeographic.co.uk/science-and-technology/2020/04/pandemic-giving-people-vivid-unusual-dreams-heres-why [accessed 12 January 2021]

[65] Sydney Shep wrote this about the nineteenth-century publishing industry. Sydney Shep, 'Culture of Print: Materiality, Memory, and the Rituals of Transmission', *Journal of New Zealand Literature* 28 (2010), pp. 183–210.

gap in the history of poetic responses to crises, most of which, like most poems themselves, are by singular poets. In some ways, we hope these collaborative poems might (at least metaphorically) suggest that we are living shared lives – that collaboration, at the personal and communal level, both, is the only way to survive.

§

This introduction has come together in a comparable way to some of the collaborations in this book: it tells one version of a 'story', and is the collaborative work of two independent voices writing to a shared objective – and across continents, as it turned out. It is the product of suggested ideas and rewrites, its objectivity filtered through the lens of two subjective perspectives. As one would expect from the nineteen pairs of writers who follow, their poetry presents an entirely diverse collection of what it means to live during the pandemic, both ranging and consolidating the emotional and aesthetic gamut. We left the remit of collaboration wide-open and readers will find a 'Collaboration Statement' by each poet-pairing after their poems, discussing their motivations and methods. In all cases, we are grateful for the poets' coming together, for their shared processes and poems. We count these works as the sorts of successes and survivals which our poets would not have come to on their own.

AC and RW
October 2020–January 2021

POETRY COLLABORATIONS

Sinéad Morrissey
&
Jan Wagner
(*trans. Iain Galbraith*)

SEALAND

I know all the colours of the sea: dirt-green, tar, mud, incarnadine.
It laps at the pillars with its million lips, yet eats so slowly
I'll be long since dishevelled by sharks, by Osedax bone-worms'
eyeless burrowing, by the time this Kingdom topples…
Fort of my heart, fort of my steel persistence
where there is only each instant, ringed and given and lit
and without alternative, carry me onto Judgement.

The washerwoman sea hangs out its mists like laundry.
Dolphins, distant shipping. I made my wife a Princess
but she rarely visits. She has flashy miraculous teeth
and loves to be photographed. Clouds. Contrails. Stars.
E Mare Libertas. I fret over inheritance like Henry.
Even the gun deck reeks of freedom – no sliver
of land in sight from the rust-eaten lookout. Sunrise, sunset,

sunrise, sunset: the days contains their replicas
which they kindly unfurl: meals out of mess-tins, admin, horizon-
scanning, sleep so deep and faceless I've reverted to factory
settings by morning. The flag of the world's smallest country
snaps in the wind and I dream of a football team.
As I jog the lovely contours of the bullseye helipad
in ever decreasing circles, happiness happens.

APPROACHING INCHKEITH

…and provided them with everything they would need for their nourishment, food, drink, fire and candle, clothes, and all other kinds of necessities needed by man or woman. He was desirous to discover what language the children would speak when they came of proper age.
　　　　　　　　　　　Robert Lindsay of Pitscottie,
　　　　　　　　　　　　The Historie and Chronicles of Scotland

two untainted by sin and a maid
mute from birth. it's a quip of the sort
to kick off some alehouse yarn
or legend of a saint. away to larboard
the roar of the surf, to the fore the storm-worn
cliffs and lass whose stub of a palate,

the moment she tries to speak, flaps about
like a herring dancing on the mole.
'wooded island' – more like a clod the lord,
bored with creation, flung away, a mile
of loneliness and haar, unredeemed, as forlorn
as a seabed wreck. and then this sky of slate.

speech to me is after the crossing when i hold
my fare in my fist or yell ashore to a friend
to catch my dock line. the name we call
a thing is like the thing, i think, while the wind
of the west hoists another tattered gull
above this fathomless realm of cold and salt.

but how will they speak, first to the maid,
then to anyone else? like breakers, tongues of angels,
a crackle of embers, storms, the peal of distant
bells on the breeze? will one scrunch like pebbles
under foot on a beach, while the second,
like this scraggy goat, utters an occasional bleat?

The Iron Room

This roof is so fine
So sheetmetal-thin
it brings God close
as a shiver as a
shudder turns all weathers
into God's Reminder
when it rains God
drums His thumbs
when it snows He fleeces us
blue & breathless

Without bricks or beams
to hold Him further off
His sheer love funnels
down enveloping us
so when we pray
we pray inside
the cold white heat of Him
there is no interloper
our mouths are awash
with sin & vinegar

I know two stand
in the field at the mill
in the tabernacle
God is under my breast-
bone but can't tell who
my blood my white-
knuckled heart in all
that feathered rushing
will be snatched and who
myself apart

TRAVEL IN TIMES OF PESTILENCE
for Sinéad Morrissey

I

you too have heard of white crosses
on doors, have seen last week's
postings in tatters on fences
like sheep's wool aflutter in the wind.

small groups of peasants, their gaze
chewing you up like cud beside the fields
of sunflowers in early autumn – black-browed, stricken,
defeated armies, orderly retreats.

as dusk falls the taverns begin
to hover, tied to their lanterns
a foot above the ground – you hear
the revellers squawking like breeding colonies,
the quacks with quicksilver
and preachers growing out of their boxes
like hairy, exotic plants.

the crows' lung balloons
over the tillage and collapses
to a dot of carrion.

is this salvation or merely a pitfall?
will the earth have room for us all?

II

maps are still to be had
but seem not to match the country.
a single territory, two nations:
those already sick, and those not yet.

what times are these, and barely a day past
since we crept into each new sunrise

like bees into bindweed blossom!
it's all processions now, cathedrals thronging
and shops shuttered with night:
only vinegar and bibles booming.

it's the signs and details you need to watch,
on the hafts of axes the freshest notch,
an opening window,
stray lights in the early hours.

passes, testimonials, letters of transit –
papers that alone, unrolled,
could extend from a to b.

choose lodgings where few people go.
keep two steps ahead of your shadow.

III

the roof of this coach must be timbered
in oak, so muffled
are the sparrows' cries, but they are here,

and pull the embroidered curtain
aside to see the scarecrows
and circus wagons, meadow mist and hamlets,
the eagle-owl nailed to a barn
like some set of theses, a pamphlet.
what heaven bestows upon you is silence
in thick flakes – embroidery of a greater kind.

now and then by the wayside, a dead horse
with its belly open, its organs' organ
within. our coachman must have
dined on cabbage, cursing from his box:
one way's blocked, the town no longer
exists, the other route's a risk.

consider the aster:
it blooms in the midst of disaster.

Original Poems by Jan Wagner

AUF INCHKEITH ZU

…and provided them with everything they would need for their nourishment, food, drink, fire and candle, clothes, and all other kinds of necessities needed by man or woman. He was desirous to discover what language the children would speak when they came of proper age.
  Robert Lindsay of Pitscottie, The Historie and Chronicles of Scotland

zwei ohne jede schuld und eine magd,
die von geburt an stumm ist – andernorts
der erste satz von kneipenanekdoten
oder von heiligenlegenden. backbord
das gischtgebrüll, voraus die sturmbenagten
klippen und die magd, der, wenn sie etwas sagt

oder zu sagen scheint, der gaumenstummel
im mund springt wie ein hering auf der mole.
„waldige insel" – eher der letzte brocken,
den gott gelangweilt fortwarf, eine meile
von einsamkeit und nebel, ungeborgen
wie wracks am grund. und dieser schieferhimmel.

sprache ist, wenn ich danach mein fährgeld
in händen halte, wenn mir eine faust
den seemannsknoten knüpft. wie etwas heißt,
entspricht ihm, denke ich, derweil ein west-
wind weitere zerfetzte möwen hisst
auf diesem tiefen reich aus salz und kälte.

wie werden sie sich äußern, vor der magd,
dann aller welt? mit engelszungen, brandungsrauschen?
knacken von glut, gewitter, dem geläute
weit weg bei gutem wind? wird einer knirschen
wie strandkies unterm fuß, während der zweite
wie diese abgezehrte ziege meckert?

DAS REISEN IN ZEITEN DER PEST
für Sinéad Morrissey

I

auch du hast gehört von den weißen kreuzen
auf türen, kennst die aushänge
von letzter woche, abgerissen am zaun
wie schafwolle im wind.

in grüppchen die bauern, die dich
mit blicken wiederkäuen vor den feldern
aus sonnenblumen im frühherbst – schwarz, gebeugt,
geschlagene heere, rückzugsmanöver.

sobald es dämmert, beginnen die schenken
ein stück überm boden zu schweben
an ihren lampions – du hörst
die feiernden, kreischend wie brutkolonien.
die quacksalber, ihr quecksilber,
und prediger, die aus kisten wachsen
wie haarige, exotische pflanzen.

die krähenlunge hat sich aufgebläht
über dem acker, fällt zusammen
in einem pünktchen aas.

ist dies die rettung oder eine falle?
und wird die erde reichen für uns alle?

II

die karten gibt es noch,
doch scheint das land nicht mehr zu passen.
ein hoheitsgebiet, zwei völker:
die kranken und die es noch nicht sind.

was für zeiten, gestern noch,
als man in jeden neuen morgen kroch
wie eine hummel in die windenblüte!

nun prozessionen, volle dome
und läden, verrammelt mit nacht:
nur bibeln und essig boomen.

du mußt auf zeichen achten, auf details,
die frischesten kerben im schaft des beils,
ein fenster, das sich öffnet,
die irrenden lichter am morgen.

passierscheine, atteste, dokumente –
papier, das aufgefaltet
allein von a nach b gelangen könnte.

wähle zum schlafen das einsamste haus.
bleib deinem schatten zwei schritte voraus.

III

die decke dieser kutsche muß aus eiche
gezimmert sein, so dumpf
klingt das geschrei der spatzen, doch es gibt sie,

und ziehst du den gestickten vorhang
zur seite, siehst du vogelscheuchen
und zirkuswagen, wiesendampf und dörfer,
den uhu, angenagelt an die scheune
wie irgendwelche thesen, ein pamphlet.
was dir der himmel schenkt, ist schweigen
in dichten flocken – die größere stickerei.

am wegrand ab und zu ein totes pferd
mit offenem bauch, die eingeweideorgel
darin. der kutscher hat zum mittag
wohl kohl gegessen, flucht von seinem bock:
ein weg blockiert, die stadt nicht länger
vorhanden, jene route ungewiß.

denk: es blüht die aster
mitten im desaster.

COLLABORATION STATEMENT
Sinéad Morrissey & Jan Wagner

I've been enjoying Jan Wagner's poetry ever since I heard him read at the Winchester Poetry Festival in 2016 (where his poem about a tea bag proved unforgettable, and where I also heard Iain Galbraith and Karen Leeder wage scintillating linguistic battle in a Poetry Translation Duel hosted by Sasha Dugdale). Just before lockdown in Spring this year, I was delighted to welcome Jan to Newcastle to read with Charlotte Van den Broeck – though even then I don't think either of us had any idea how the rest of 2020 would actually unfold. When the invitation came to write a Covid-19-inspired sequence in collaboration with another poet, I was intrigued to see how a poetic conversation with Jan would actually run.

I knew I wanted to start with Sealand – a derelict naval fort between England and France 'claimed' by Roy Bates in 1966 as the world's smallest country (you can buy Sealand coinage and flags off the Internet). As the poem unfolded, it became as much about Brexit as about lockdown: an ironic commentary on the kind of jubilant dead-end afforded by breaking ourselves up into smaller and smaller national units. When Jan responded with an even grimmer story of isolationism, one of great cruelty and arrogance, inspired by religious fervour, I knew I wanted to internalise the kind of violence described in the poem in order to explore "the true language of God" as a language of self-laceration. I had come across the phrase "The Iron Room" in a memoir about being raised in the Plymouth Brethren, and so I started with a speaker inside a church with a thin roof, with God just above it, breathing down. The only place to go in this poem is incoherence, of selfhood, and of speech. I think Jan's final poem, spring-boarded off my tin tabernacle, is a tour-de-force. The authority of the historical voice, grounded in riveting and entirely unexpected details, is mesmeric: in it we get to listen to the pandemic's darkest possible consequences, set to resonate like a bell from Doomsday.

SM

Ever since Sinéad's first collection appeared in the nineties, I have been an enthusiastic reader of her poetry. Occasionally we met, now and again we shared the stage at a poetry reading, and all of these get-togethers were delightful – so when Sinéad suggested that we should cooperate on this poetic-pandemic exchange, there was not a moment of hesitation on my part.

When contemplating certain contemporary subject matters (especially those so grievous that heart and mind and language struggle to come to terms with them), an indirect approach often seems more fertile to me – knowing or hoping that such a slant angle, distorting as it may seem at first, may result in a clearer view of what is happening after all. Fortunately, Sinéad suggested right at the start that for her, too, the detour may be the most promising route. Her poem on the curious "Sealand" (which I had not encountered before) confirmed this beautifully, and it seemed right to respond to it with another off-shore location, a scene still more remote historically (similar stories about newborns being separated from society in order to find out about man's original language are related in other parts of the world as well, but it seemed a matter of politeness to stay as close as possible to both Newcastle and the Suffolk coast). In our second round – Sinéad yet again setting the standard with "The Iron Room" – I reacted in a less straightforward manner: not an island in exchange for an island this time, but more hidden references and innuendos – the three-part structure, to begin with, Sinéad's very first line ("This roof…") finding its echo in the opening verse of my own third part, the reemergence of the vinegar and, of course, heaven expressing itself with its precipitations.

Projects such as this one with its predefined frame and time scale can turn out to be burdensome in that an enormous amount of (self-made) pressure can arise in the process (no diamonds without pressure, however). In this case the exchange turned out, as hoped, to be pure pleasure and no pressure at all. Thanks, then, once again for this idea, the invitation, and my gratitude, as always, to Iain Galbraith who, with his precise and musical translations from German into English, laid the foundation for our cooperation.

JW

Carol Leeming & Rakhshan Rizwan

SOME THINGS THAT NEVER SEEM TO FAIL ME

Some things that never seem to fail me
hearty spiced meat rice piping comfort

what I think I should do I don't emphatically
to exult in a staid inertia a vicarious thrill

a bath soporific with fine essential oils
frankincense notes solace of lavender

a sex toy humming bird tips divinely
my whines spasm floridly psychedelic

blurry rambles along too quiet streets
suddenly a stranger's furtive rusty smile

walks parks filled with elated trees grass
hiccupping streams boastful struts of birds

imaginary friends to walk me late at night
drink lucent stars thirsty to swallow inky sky

fervent prayers danced night into day
ancestral viridian songs with ululations

peppery music fills glaring voids at home
tunes play full-bodied motion to gladden

missed loves' heartstrings strum fondly
absence mints most kindly all of my tears

a glazed memory winds into my view
filigrees of a lover's succulent caresses

a room of faux quietude disarms my soul
solitary pursuits gratify as studied reveries

a new found fetish for my hair skin nails
profound novel self-love of an epic scale

left to my own devices at home I am coyly naive
dressing up mirror says the clothes my fantasies fit

habitual escapism in films my choice to steal time
flickering squared eyes offer criticisms unsurpassed

a phone computer of cobalt pixels shoots staves of love
I dematerialise materialise into rooms so I am there

to hear quiet isn't silent as dead people live close by
speaking to loquacious silence it secrets *duppy* dances

a recipe for grief: recall all your lost one's witless banter
keep memories of stupid things loved ones did til' you roar

a recipe for anger: for venal government homicidal lies
curse guttural expletives at tv rise drink camomile tea

a pair of stern knitting needles clicks criss-crossing
I like a *tricoteuse* do banish all dread to instil calm

be an *arriviste* domestic goddess culinary conjuror
facebook eats my photos before I gorge luscious food

mute pillows willingly mercilessly punched or tightly held
kitchen utensils broken thrown forcefully bashed relieves

alchemy: sing loudly tremulously for potent mood boost
to dance solo or with a partner causes ecstatic flying

to revel: mysterious allure kinky mask sex appeals
as a world drags pauses with aforethought and effect

a recipe for depression: sleep long plumb pearly dreams
wake up say *carpe diem carpe diem* till you laugh loudly

to immerse in seas of words pleasure seeking in books
take in fluent chapters by the writers' airs of imagination

imagine voices faces family friends their cheery chorus
unseen lines tracing bonds holding a space that is me.

whines: Jamaican Patois African Caribbean dance circular thrusting hip/pelvic movements.

tricoteuse: marginalised women who knitted at the side of guillotine executions French Revolution.

duppy: Jamaican Patois / African Caribbean spirit of the dead.

The Disappearing Act

Elizabeth Siddal, the Sunday painter,
model for the Pre-Raphaelites,
Razia Sultana, Iltutmish's daughter,
Mileva Maric, Einstein's wife,
How do we prepare for this impending erasure?
Alice Munro told us to,
write short stories
as we watched the babies,
Susan B. Anthony
said ride a damn bicycle
ladies, it's just better, more efficient,
Rise! Maya Angelou commanded us,
it's the problem
without a name,
as per my friend, Friedan,
I call it: a fast-growing tumour in the marrow,
let's catch it early,
the doctor says, to the ghostly x-ray,
the tumour, the shape of a seed,
becoming the civilization,
amassing mass,
as we remain mired in the days,
serving ghee, cream
and our dreams to the
hungry universe, the invisible
economy of women,
here, see, this work,
I pinpoint to the field of my cyclical efforts,
the tended to, the produce, the children,
the spoils, the order,
Here, here, I cannot stop
talking about it, the quicksand of oblivion,
a terrible sleep is taking us over, obsolescence,
no escaping it, bound to our homes,
outside, the sky a terrible shade of yellow,
each breath is ash, The Golden Gate
Bridge disappears behind a plume of smoke,

I draw in air, to find
rest, respite, but in my sleep,
I hear a multitude of voices,
raised as I am by centuries of vanished women,
their mongrel tongue is my language,
they begin singing: 'shrink yourself, be less,
grow closer to your ribs, become manageable, small,
be bite-sized, be nothing,
be the antidote to the animosity,
the vaccine to the vacuousness,
swallow the sadness,
mellow the melancholia
untangle the unsolvable,
tinker with it with your teeth,
melt into the economy,
that is the solution
to market forces,
pathogenic invasions
climate change,
wildfires, unemployment,
racism, keep asking
where it hurts,
keep hugging *your huddled masses*,
keep finding solutions in your bodies
keep vanishing in numbers,
unaccountable, keep disappearing
in names, unnameable, keep
taking falls, for all of us,'
I shush the voices; they quieten down,
with my hands, I turn my skin into a field
of shea butter, exorcise from it the residual histories,
then, I move down the nape of my neck,
deep into to my shoulder blades,
which stretch outwards to the sky, like Icarus
mid-flight, I carefully untie each knot
each call to sacrifice,
and set every tortuous contortion
of muscle memory,
free.

COLLABORATION STATEMENT
Carol Leeming and Rakhshan Rizwan

Meeting someone over Zoom for the first time can be a strange, discombobulating experience, but in this case, it turned into something quite seamless and enjoyable. We had a natural rapport from the very beginning, taking time to absorb the political usurpations in our midst, exchanging notes on our everyday Covid routines and comparing the morose politics of our respective countries. We were both experiencing a sense of ennui, a plague-induced state of inertia, when we initially started speaking and had been struggling with the writing process. Gradually, the subject matter of our as-yet-unrealized poems, began to organically take shape in our conversations, which revolved around the different spaces we occupied (Leicester/San Ramon), the global politics of race and the Black Lives Matter movement, the shared histories of the empire and the post-colonies, the psychic temporalities produced by Covid-19 and the home as a liminal space where women are restricted especially during the pandemic. Even in this early stage of the collaborative process we could see the emergence of a shared transnational feminist perspective and we agreed that this would strongly inform the content of our first draft. Our poems situate the body as the epicentre for both loneliness and connection, testifying to the resistive powers of pleasure especially in moments of biological and political crisis.

George Szirtes
&
Alvin Pang

Past Time

We sigh the word 'again'
as if it were a new thing
like rediscovering rain,
an endless reckoning
with our sense of ending.

We are waiting for the train
to arrive before it has left.
We're singing the refrain
while music comes adrift
and trains refuse to shift.

We think to breathe and weigh
the sunlight as it falls
on grass swept through the day
by wind like distant bells
or anything that tolls.

Dear friend, the words between
the silence rearrange
the various shades of green
though nothing seems to change,
so even grass is strange.

*

Nothing seems to change
and nothing seems to move;
the heart ebbs out of range:

it craves a sea to love
but all there is, is groove

and tolerable drain
and mud raked over coals
for heat. But still we strain
to sing, to brave the shoals.
The minutes claim their tolls.

The hours pay their keep.
The tables turn and plead
for unreserved sleep.
The still extracts a fee:
free time is never free.

Old Leonard had it right:
that everything is cracked.
I had to slough my sight
to gain this smarting fact.
Each day I cannot act

is one forfeit, astray,
misspent. A page turned.
But what is there to say
with time? What earned?
And to what blind end?

This rhyme is delay.

*

We are only delaying autumn, not cancelling it,
Autumn will not be postponed. Or not for long.
Leaves that are preparing to fall will reconsider
their position and will make a statement
in due course. Birds have continued to mate
and the rate of egg production has not fallen,
nor have the leaves. Birds wings continue to beat.

The position with hearts is equally assuring.
They too continue to beat and have not been cancelled
though some may experience an inevitable delay.
This is the language and these are the terms
in which we negotiate delay and postponement.
Be assured that nothing has been cancelled.
Our punctuation is in place, grammar is on our side.
So now there is only autumn to prepare for.

*

I'm thinking how here we reckon
Our days without the seasons' clock:
pendulous Fall, Winter's white tock.

I suppose what we do is carry on
Until caught, invariably, by surprise:
May's loud heat, December's lush skies.

Today an unseasonable gloom
Has thrilled an afternoon:
A year-end storm come much too soon.

Heaven reduced to a waiting room.
A Ragnarok thrum. The bawl of a jet.
It's August, but not September yet.

The schoolward course is test-bound,
Rung-stepped, an almanac of hoops.
The Financial Year, implacable, loops

Onto itself: Finds us but is never found
Wanting. Another while, another clinical scan.
Man hands worriment to man

In a sealed plain envelope.
Dental visits. Barber stops. We take
Circling as certainty of line. Break

As mark of headway. Of hope
That things pass: that passing might be
Passable, welcome, light, free.

*

What is it to come to an end? It is not this
stream of words with its arbitrary stops
and hesitations. That could go on for ever
or whatever 'for ever' means. There is no doubt
that sentences exist and that lines end
because we make them end. Listen to the drip
and drawl, the drudgery of it; the gripe
and growl of it as it passes through time.
The clothes on the line are in high spirits
like can-can dancers kicking up their legs.
The clouds muse on them and withdraw
into ever deeper recesses of contemplation.
My tongue is sore with speaking. My throat is dry.
I trudge through endless deserts of syntax
to arrive at this wordless deserted fort
where some foreign legion briefly fetched up
and entered memory through the back door of film.

There was no dialogue then, only film
waiting for a soundtrack, for its version of cut-up,
time's own fan fiction. where we built a fort
out of whatever it affords, its walls of syntax
crumbling. We joked about it, admired its dry
humour, and its thirst for contemplation.
We said we'd spend night there and then withdraw
into a sense of the local on its own last legs.
What are we then, sentences or spirits?
What happened to us, what drags us through time
with its own limited versions of growl and gripe?
Listen again. Do you hear it now? The drip, drip, drip
of water seeking its own vessels and an end
to waiting. There is no certainty without doubt,
and doubt, no doubt, could carry on for ever.

Let's imagine here is where it stops,
here in mid-sentence, or a place like this.

*

Why do we sentence
ourselves to this refusal
of silence, these beats

of idle fingers
upon the wall of a page?
I come back to this:

Sometimes one world thins
enough to hear another,
the faintest echo

of what might yet be
or what perhaps is, elsewhere.
A life we can't touch

yet half-remember;
a second movement, a next,
a continuing.

An ear pressed against
the shadows of cinemas
and churches, asleep

to its own slumber.
Leave the boy be, muttering
to unseen spirits,

his black, tousled hair
greying in the skittish light,
dreaming of waking,

his palms clutching air
as at the thread of a song
leading him homeward,

the music made in
being, being with; knowing
as a kind of end.

*

What news of the world?
– From my part of the country
the wind and the sea.

And what news in yours?
– Just dark clouds growing darker
and the sound of things

falling. - Falling far?
– As if for ever. And time
slowly retreating.

– Then there is still time.

COLLABORATION STATEMENT
George Szirtes & Alvin Pang

We first met in Norwich at an international conference in 2012; we quipped and made each other laugh and became acquainted with each other's work. From time to time we had opportunities – albeit all too few – to spend time together: in Malaysia, in Singapore, and across the UK. We found between us an easy, natural friendship, as well as a poetic meeting of minds. Over the years, we had discussed wanting to collaborate in writing, and this project was a prime occasion. Our collaboration began with a short ten-line poem by George, itself part of a daily poetic journal of the UK's first lockdown. Writing poems back and forth in response to each other, our correspondence took in our respective circumstances and moods, socially, physically and mentally. We moved with the progress of the disease, beginning with a sort of haiku-like form and then adopting various forms of verse as we proceeded (and as the year evolved). In registering and exploring the times in which we find ourselves living, our exchange has stretched well beyond the stipulated four pages. It continues even now, and we hope to complete a book's worth of material from this duet.

Vahni Capildeo
&
Vivek Narayanan

[what land does not wear
the sound of the sea
then you reach a place
dry of the sea's sound]

[my heart has no wealth
it washes no land
in this it cannot
be named a woman's]

Elements of the Mask

cut from conches smooth and shiny bangles   loosen every day on the wrist
     unsleeping   eyes wet with aloneness
         stuck here we'll   escape to over there
first rise up and live   my heart
     before the hemp chaplets   of the Vadukars
   beyond Katti   honourable land of many spears
     further into the country   of unknown languages
     thinking how to reach   the place where he is

[from the *Kuruntokai*, ancient Tamil anthology
of 4–8 line poems: no. 11, Maamoolanar]

The place where he is with underground cables
    hates itself as consequence
Too much luxury air nourishment income   Some
    in waiting   Escarpments over dizzying
siesta When grace finally came
to you the plains   aflame The man
there with his cheap blood   The deaths
in every unmarked house vanished   mated
with profiles And hovered above it hour
after happy hour meals in the making or
on the table   comes to us so innocuous   long as art
which too comes to an end   Spoken
like curious prophecy   Was how
I bought my way across this border
in the air cocoon or maybe back of
sea creature   The customs little man you know I know
shrugging at all the customs parading through
his gate   The stamp little man you know I know
stamping away his decrees   But most of all
the paper with handwritten address
that brought you brought you
to a door   Re-membering that white dress
now
*

the face of the family pharmacist
duskens with condemnation
so does his assistant's   a word of goodbye
is more welcome than welcome
and not forthcoming   bitter
your departure to inexistent
choices   bitter your choice
of unknowable friends

there are many people
who have not seen land
from the air

the border is guarded by men
who address me in the language
they think I speak they think you speak
and neither of us can speak   and we are not
travelling together
you get through all right? you get through?

If we know water
If we know water not by wetness
but by our change in footing
If we know water only by light flowing
strongly as a changing change –
It is not new, either
that people kill when they come out their houses
kill when they breathe outwith their houses
on others   it is not new
that people stay inside if they have houses
You're not protected
Your eyes are too big for your mask
They can tell you are smiling
Running in a mask   the cotton flows
back into the scoop of lips   dark breath is water

The way the rocks write the water
   with the water
  the way the road
    devours the fig tree
   in its scrutiny of pattern
  Each night I walk
into the dark thinking of him

                    Land
                    Land is if
                    Land is if we know
                    it by the way it pours
                    from the lower sky –

                    to leave to kill
                    to reach yours to kill

                    Your eyes all I remember
                    your mask has no character

                    are you sitting in the fig tree
                    spiritual spy
                    pulling out your own tongue
                    over which you'll escape

no longer the great master
just another boy
on the dance floor
When gone in his lying cloud
I'm useless to myself

Your feet too slow to outrun the ill
The ridges of the body
and its farther valleys to see the grain of the overbridge
only in shadow   lobbed sound of cars
   Can't tell you the guilty joy
in reaching river   in stillness of its lurk
enveloped   plastered in fortune
Rings   the endless telephone in the minister's office
We'll plant new fields   feed the fish new
crumbs of bone   Not the creature terror that
matters   but the vast cover makes
tell me what you want to hear
say it back to me

bridging
disco ball wisdom
and the absence of internet
which is normal   which is
normal

I offer you a fist of crystal
you scrape salt from it

honourable to edible
I dredge the mud to host

What I want to hear from you
is that a piece of honeycomb

is strapped to everything you eat
and that a menstruating ritual dancer
carries out the repairs in your apartment block
and what are the bad basics
of everyone else's published book
I want to hear a gooseflesh acknowledgements page
outpaced by pine trees
and a dossier of disbelief
in the full moon that zoomed out
of the whirling class
that whirled out of the zoom class
in a clear visor
with a scroll in his mouth
and little white dogs under his feet
Tell me how to speak to you
other than from eclipse or dreaming
when half the life I live is blotted out
and the other half belongs
to a family of denials
in which I am a walking pillar of attrition
offered a cushion of cactus seed?
The art of the teeth which came back
after loss and decay

Some wonders must
still exist

across his ballooning skirts

(With half an Oxford Shorter in my arms:)
    Or hadst thou waited… Thy spirit
should have filled its crescent sphere

The born relative is the enemy
    it cannot separate itself from you
Only friends shall be relatives
    from crescent spheres split open
And certain faiths that come in twos

is a more than human act
in an other than human mouth.
Tell me how you are
not like that
Tell me
how are you…

She fell and hit herself
  on the pavement
Months into the bedsore
  she was gone with her sleep
Forty years he said I've not
  been alone in this apartment
Head office came with that bad call
  suddenly they were all
kings and queens without empires
Head of State meantime busy with the lab testing
  Revived his corpse on a Monday morning
  still in a coma while
  his fans immolated themselves
Remember it so clearly from the news
  some forty years ago
Mother she struggles to cope with itself

their critical silt overrisen
  sliden into gentle senility
  eased by supplements and additives

take responsibility:
'the glass broke?'
no you broke the glass
broken yourself upon the way
to no mothering
it is a pointless journey
dying in your sleep

dreaming you were young
dreaming you were you
  young

all the blood must go somewhere
I hear they drink it   subtly
gross bodies   imbibe subtle bodies
startle   at an internal cocktail party
back to youth   anyway I know
they're gone

                              examine yourself

violent triage

I had a liquorice syllabus
                              for Halloween

raise your hand and say   present

is your name   ghost or gift

ghosts are boring
                              crushed leaves

still alive still awake Terrified
    a bad translation might have slipped her lips
        Father in his lonely boat
rowing rowing away   Sometimes stopped for hours
            to drift and wave
        Sister with full marks
Neighbors will not build
    their outhouse this year
If see a man walking below
    must become him
So many of them that
I am vanished if ever to speak

Into the classroom they arrive
    reclining on their palanquins
Into the classroom they arrive
    in yards or unlit porches
Into the classroom they arrive
    in their stark prison-white rooms
Into the classrooms they arrive
    with sandwiches in hand
Into the classroom they arrive
with dubbed and accidental names

Into the classroom they arrive
    undimmed yet by false fortune
Into the classroom they arrive
    carrying their toys with them

        rise into the back of the nostrils
        smell of the living

                    and no food

A tree as yellow as an egg was shaking itself
called by the name omniscience.
You have to meet me by that tree
according to the terms indoors no longer
and the links are high wind.
I cannot carry a coat on my back
to meet the shaking yellow oval of omniscience
I cannot carry anything on my back
and write   I can only write
inside the covers of books   I have not read
and in which I haven't written anything.
"My mask protects you. Your mask
protects me." I choke on the half of it
among the citizenry of meeting without completion.
Your face is your fortune.
Fortune is a risk.
I have to see your face   I have to

        in the intercommunal garden
        not all rocks were smooth

            one at the heptamerous shrine imbued
                with ashes made sacred

                citizenry that finds its limbs like
                    a stumbling toddler

                        Your face is all I have
                        your face all I have
                            to face   to have

jointless under
the glomerate jojoba

fearless volving the seam
Here we go Here we go let the water

ever find us where we go

take your risk   and then I'll
take your fortune.   They said this
long before the present   only now
I know the stitching.   They were working
under the moon   under those trees
which now are dancing   one like fire
one like something taller than itself.
What is taller than itself?   I turned
my back to the sea   to look for the tree
called by the name omniscience
egg-bright, tremulous and having escaped
the ritual infusion of the moony human.
You should never turn your back to the sea.
Waves intend to be taller than themselves.
That is what is meant by   impending

COLLABORATION STATEMENT
Vahni Capildeo & Vivek Narayanan

Vahni and I know each other's work well and speak fairly often on the phone, but we hadn't communicated in this seemingly 'slant epistolary' manner before. Very little of the process was (or needed to be) discussed before or during, so I can't speak to her experience. COVID and the concurrent disaster of its mismanagement by fascist-leaning and/or authoritarian governments everywhere is certain to leave a long, and long-lasting scar. For whatever it's worth, though, this also appears to be a moment that forces new connections – connections that for some reason had not yet been activated even if the technology and the means for them existed. Vahni's and my collaborative poem is perhaps like that too.

VN

Vivek and I met via email in 2008 or thereabouts, without any personal introduction or connexion. Vivek had been researching poets to invite to contribute to *Almost Island* and take part in several days of conversation in Delhi. His seemingly tireless, piercing, roaming intelligence from early on has made the best of the potential of the technologies that can connect (though they also veil) us. While his global knowledge, which reaches far back in time as well as constantly crossing space, occasionally daunts me, I could think of nobody better with whom to address the current moment. Our consciousness, and the poetic forms appropriate to it, are transforming during the pandemic. Yet discontinuity is not the whole story. There are continuities with our recent and remote past. Separation, shock, yearning, and encounter remain as human as ever. From meditating on Vivek's translation of an ancient Tamil text, I started to dream the voices of characters speaking from violent or extreme moments. Somehow, these imaginary people remained aware of themselves as part of nature and able to seek for their fellows. Hence the interweaving which we offer here.

VC

Rory Waterman
&
Togara Muzanenhamo

Burrs

We are turning into ghosts here. The days mirror each other.
Silence sits flat like a stone on the horizon. Muting everything.
The house is cold and dark and quiet as a cave. My daughter
wakes up much later than usual. And as I am seated, writing
this to you, she's still in bed – her body clock adjusted three
weeks back. After schools closed, she was so happy to be free

from the early morning rush – dressing as she ate breakfast,
the neighbours' dogs barking and cars revving and speeding out
of wrought iron gates, traffic flooding streets as the sun cast
its eye through the kitchen window where my wife would shout
For Christ's sake we're going to be late. Faucets running.
Keys lost then found. Doors slamming. The general chaos of leaving.

All these things my daughter now comments on with a hint
of regret. Though she's happy to go to bed late and wake up late –
though she's adjusted to the quiet – there's just one complaint
that constantly drags at her heels like an invisible weight. Eight
year olds, she insists, should get out and play with their friends.
She's also beginning to tire of asking when all of this will end.

I leave for my mother's, fleet through ghost suburbs and into
my plotted and pieced homeland. And, yes, 'When will this end?'
she says, gesturing a happy hug across her yard. Then 'Let's go!'
and I follow her command, her boots, round the fields, the bends
in countless hedges, on a route she's treaded daily, from budding
hawthorn to bulging haws, stopping to 'gosh!' at anything

*that moves, or to lift her binoculars, often frantically missing
whatever it was: a kestrel trembling on cloud, a green woodpecker
fanning back to the copse. She wants to show me something.
This is why I am here: love without touch, to risk her health for
our health. The hay is baled, our calves pimpled with burdock burrs.
And, worlds away, riots have broken out again, I tell her,*

*slipping my bastard phone away, sorry, as silently we decide
not to navigate what we think, even for one another. We're
on the edge of the woods now, near a stable, derelict beside
a brick-strewn, dimpled lawn that was a country house. 'Not far'
she says, proud, then grabs for my hand as she misjudges
a style, retracts in a blink, tumbles hard to the mud.*

Driven by necessity, we pack up and head out to the farm.
The road's a wide ribbon of tar with a cautious stream of cars.
Silence still reigns. The morning sun falls across my forearm.
The passenger seat is empty, my daughter in the back, her tears
long dried after refusing to wear the mask – eyes fixed to the screen
of her tablet. In a calm voice, she says she's never seen

so many men with guns as we drive away from the first of three
checkpoints. The city falls back with its suburbs and townships –
farmland expanding in dry blond swathes of grass where barley
and wheat once stood in stiff green regiments with faint slips
of mist layered above needled awns. Hard to imagine after two
decades, wild grasslands knotted with cockle burrs. Equally hard to

grasp how the months to come will ultimately define an age
within this century. And at the final checkpoint I hand over my pass
and the soldier's eye lifts from the document's final page –
then commands I roll the car's rear window down and the glass
sinks to reveal a child wrapped in a duvet, masked and quiet.
His eye falls cold on her not fearing the virus, but the coming riots.

*But she rights herself, quietly, still fit enough, and on we go. And
we are not to talk about it – I know that. But eventually she talks
around it: 'I'm getting old now. I want to enjoy life while I can' –
and is this it? – as she leads me along a fence by a wood. We walk*

*in single file through tendrilled nettles, to where an unclipped strand
of fence wire bellies towards the turf. She doesn't try for my hand*

*this time – and makes it. The treetops ride the breeze a little
but everything is stillness down here. A shotgun cartridge cracks
beneath her toe, a blackbird hops from a stump to scuff leaflitter.
And she peers long-range like a squirrel, grass-stained back
to me, then points: 'This way'. And as we go, I tell her about you,
this poem. After all, she always wants to know the things I do,*

*so let's try that. 'Zimbabwe! What's it like there?' she says, placing
'there' in a mental map of a region she's traversed much more
extensively, but I know what she means, what this now means. We face
sculpted rock I recognise from childhood, that we must have come for,
but I won't say I've been here. 'Few cases anywhere until June. Parts
are now on the usual curve.' I cast a stone. It sails like a line on a chart.*

The midday sun is warm and pale shadows stain the earth at our
heels. This is the good air – the air away from the city. The view
from the homestead is nothing but rhodes grass rolling out the hour-
long walk to the neighbour's – well, the last neighbour we knew.
My daughter immediately rips off her mask, kicks off her shoes
and runs through the rose garden for the swing, heels and toes

in full momentum even before I begin to unpack the car. Yes.
This is the good air – rinsed, cleansed of everything but the chain
of the swing slightly creaking above a lone dove's call – the ease
of breath reassured with the next intake that comes easier again
and again – until breathing is forgotten and the senses accept
each sensory gift given back to something within that slept

with fear – only to reawaken and shudder, blistered with emotion.
As I stand there immersed in this, the front door of the farmhouse
opens and my mother appears in the jamb. And it's not caution
that roots us in place. The mandated distance is a comfortable excuse
as we greet each other from afar. She steps back into the shadows
of the corridor. I lift the bags and enter and my daughter follows,

and we find our room as we left it months ago – the mirror above
the dresser hazed with dust, the curtains closed. Evening passes
with a sharp dry wind. And as dawn approaches, the corrugated roof
stiffens with frost and creaks. My daughter is fast asleep as I dress.
Stepping out, I check my phone. The air is cold. The sky bruised blue.
From my palm I read the morning news. Harare Under Curfew.

We gawp into the puzzle of a limestone lime-green fountain,
a lead pipe stub in its bowl, a handful of dirt. Webs of ivy follow
its contours still. And, over there, the old rope swing. I'll try it again –
but who is this now, emerging from the leaf-waving shadows?
'Are you lost? You can't be here' he says, pointing at the new farmhouse
we hadn't noticed: bright brick over privet. Stiffly, he guides us out.

And as we trudge on home I check my phone again, see your email.
Harare's a ghost town, I tell her. Patrolled. Silent. Under curfew.
Shouldn't I have known? But our news is our news. America's as well.
On the landing page this morning: another daubed, dented statue.
Crowds facing off somewhere. Burned lots. BLM. Back the Blue.
All foreign round here. A kestrel twitches, dips behind some bales –

too quick. Then we're back. She gestures another hug. I gesture one too,
and slip into gear and out of her little lane, checking for her arm
in the mirror, lifting mine, sighing. Hoping to have done no harm.

COLLABORATION STATEMENT
Rory Waterman & Togara Muzanenhamo

Rory and Togara met in 2014 in Nottingham, where Togara was giving a reading at Five Leaves Bookshop. Rory had just reviewed Togara's second collection, *Gumiguru*, for the *TLS*. He had particularly enjoyed Togara's occasional method of building a setting and narrative in his poems through long-lined, loosely rhymed stanzas. When this project was conceived, he approached Togara with the suggestion that they work on a poem together. Togara had been aware of Rory's poetry from his 2013 debut collection, *Tonight the Summer's Over*, which struck him for Rory's bold use of colloquialism and well-crafted form. With this poem, both poets agreed on a structure, with Togara beginning the first section and Rory following. As the poets worked, they quickly found that two narratives were emerging and being woven together in empathy.

The poem was first published in *PN Review*.

Rachael Allen
&
Ilya Kaminsky

Contested dome and boundaries of earth,
charred remains kept away from the house,
but keep me in mind
something like an animal corpse
in your peripheral vision.
The dark field obscures me
But I'll be waving hello.
Someone takes in night air settling on a purple field.
There she goes walking,
see love move as a virus
altering preposterously
sun dappled scenery.

While People Die,
You and I Speak of Sun Dappled Scenery

in a time of pandemic you see love move as a virus
there she goes walking,

someone takes in night air settling on a purple field, yes?
But I too will be waving hello.

while the dark field obscures me.
I still don't know why I am repeating this, Rachael, I will be
waving hello.

Why are we here on this
planet friend, contested by what boundaries, what earth?

In a time of pandemic
someone takes night, someone takes, you say, but all is
taken, and night

is still here, night and air,
air settling air settling on a purple field.

Ilya, I watched myself perform
as though televised
watched the great ice shelf
sink into the blue abyss
learned about the paradise crow
on the History Channel
cartooned inaccurate drawings
led to years of misinformation.

*

I will be believed one day
if not for this performance
then perhaps my next.
What would happen if there was
a microphone installed
somewhere in this bedroom?
Yes zig-zag life of me I
cannot remember
what we talked about.

Yes, years of misinformation. Yes, zigzag of life

zigzag somewhere in this bedroom I call a planet.
What is a day

if not a human not knowing what a day is.
What is speech

if not a microphone
installed

in a skull?
What is speech, Rachael?

Yes, zigzag life
Zigzag,

Zigzag of life.

    *

Ilya, I used to look up and feel the earth
come apart in my stomach; not now.

Petri dish exclamations, your mood is,
and a hard bound hand against me
and my hands bound hard behind me, against wood.

I lived by your mood, an operational system
how overcome is the day?
Between green veils and a tendril of thought
the mapping of substance, traveling through
a waterway back and forward in time.

Tree a bit between my teeth like ancient dentistry
a bit between my teeth and you gallop me around like an animal.
Dallied pet.

What is it to love a virus
a person
a prophylactic acid, a trouble in the systemics.

How it makes it way through sinus and back again.

A Body, How It makes Its Way Through Sinus and Back Again

To sinus and back.
to sinus, and back, to sinus, to sinus and not

back.
I too used to look up and feel the earth come apart in my stomach. I,

too, lived by moods, operational systems
of a day.

Between green veils and a tendril of thought
I, too, shivered.

Traveling via
a body

which is a time machine
going about sixty seconds per minute, I too, wept.

What is it
to love a virus I know not. I don't

love a virus. I love
persons. Though each of us

is a trouble in the systemics, is a prophylactic acid,
though each

of us
only has each of us,

Rachael, and not, and not, not for long. What is it
like to riot in the municipal

architecture of a body
I do see

And while I verse
others die and while I verse lovingly others

die;
how it riots its way through sinus and back again, I see,

how we are still here, Rachael,
in this drop of sun dappled scenery, I see, we are still
here, friend.

COLLABORATION STATEMENT
Rachael Allen & Ilya Kaminsky

"They lived. They wrote. They are (or are they?) still here."

I took the liberty
and stopped it null.
I tried to live
I did not write.

Dear reader: if you need more explanation, take your idea of explanation, and slip a lit match or two in its chest-pockets.

Response in kind in an unkind time. Please unfold the pocket-book explanation and, as above, let it smoulder.

Dear reader: These are the times I don't want to make poems of. When sending two silences, wrapped in a newspaper, is enough. Times when seven line-breaks and four carnations are enough. Taking a word from a friend and giving it back, slightly limping, out of breath, but coy and cuddly, is a plenty.

And once you have the word from a friend, dunk the of poems *wrapped in news in the big-fat fryer. You can eat them, deliciously! For breakfast or lunch. Don't eat them for dinner.*

Dear reader: Let's not talk about poems for two and half minutes. Friendships are peculiar animals, too, line-breaks or no line-breaks. Silences also make drum beats. By our absences the music is conceived. Friendships are peculiar animals, too, dear reader, line-breaks or not.

I am trying to talk about food
you can talk about food
with line breaks
and a delicious slap
greasy
to music

Hey, look! it's snowing. Snow is like a huge t-shirt chewed up by a dog one poet said. Snow's transformed the avenue into a hospital, said another poet. Such are these times.

Here it snows too – fold it up – in the pocket book – and set it alight.

Zoë Skoulding
&
Yana Lucila Lema Otavalo

Song of Gulls and Hummingbirds

kunan kampa wakay sumaklla uyarin
        now your cry seems like another
kunanka tukuyllapa rinllipi kampa samay uyarinmi
        now we all hear your breath in our ears

now there are cries without tears
there's awe in our eyes
there's turquoise of fiestas
there's sea green
there's blackness of earth
silence breathing

mamaku this is your time
to run free your blood through the fields
through the lived city
through the black of a night that isn't night
through the shadow of day that fires up the sun

mamaku your name›s been in everyone›s mouth
we've put gifts of sweet fruit in your belly
we've spread holy smoke in your territory
we've flexed our feet against the ground to talk to you

now
now when life is leaving us
when pain has come to us
when our breathing's cut short
when we can't even talk to our dead

now
now when we can see your wounds bleed into our own skin
we don't want to forget your injured body
the seeds not germinated
children who are born but dying

mamaku this is your night and day at the same time
our night and day as humans too

llullu wawakunapak yakuta allichishunchuyari
      will we keep water for the newborn
ñukanchikpa kashka allpata shamukkunapak wakaychishunchuyari
      will we keep the earth for other hands
manllay pacha hipa imashina kawsanata yashkanchikchuyari
      have we thought about what comes after fear
ñukanchik mamaku ñukanchik samayta uyay tukunkacha
      will *mamaku* still hear our breath our beating hearts

*

wakay: cry of a human, animal
or bird lamenting or
speaking its own language

but how would you know if a bird
is lamenting
    or if speaking its own language
is already a lament

here the hummingbirds are weeping
with drunken laughter
high on sugar dizzily flitting
voice of needle beak pique flower
bother of wings
    have at you
        looped around again
kinti kinti   *inti*
kith and kin
          oh hummingsun

hungry gulls abandon
empty streets and benches
and call to the whole grey sky
how how how do you say this

now
who are you so far away
now
who are you and how
in the green of skies in the turquoise
         how in the black of days
will you turn on the beat of a wing

we are abandoned into birth
with these cries that name us

orphans

music as sounded skin slips into
a sort of swoon or *kinti* song
reaching into connection
an inaudible note too high to catch

    breath quivers on the wire
    when it's night and it isn't

    mothers in pixels
    mothers in leaves and light

and the speaking dead come through
their voices underground
earthed in electrical echoes

COLLABORATION STATEMENT
Zoë Skoulding & Yana Lucila Lema Otavalo

Yana started off by sending me lines originally written in Kichwa, and which she had translated into Spanish. I translated these by working from Spanish, and asking about the Kichwa. I've left in a few of the original lines so that Yana's language has its own space on the page as sound, as an interference in English, and also as a way of acknowledging translation as the incomplete, provisional process that it is. The second part of the poem is my echo of the first, refracted through Nathaniel Mackey's essay 'Sound and Sentiment, Sound and Symbol,' and bringing in my own lockdown environment on Anglesey, where I'm surrounded by gulls rather than hummingbirds. We began our collaboration at midsummer, when Inti Tayta, the paternal deity of the sun, is celebrated across Ecuador, Bolivia and Peru.

ZS

In Kichwa, *Wakay,* crying, suggests distress in humans, but singing or joy in animals or birds. The diminutive *mamaku* expresses love, care and respect; without the *ku* ending, the word would sound distant. I'm thinking not only of a human mother (and my own mother) but also the earth as mother or *allpamama*. At celebrations, women wear bright *rebozos* or shawls of turquoise, fuchsia, intense green and red. Flexing the feet is the position in which to kiss the ground, like the elders. While it might look like the Catholic gesture of kneeling, this is a way of greeting the earth. I like the songs of the smaller birds, like hummingbirds, *kinti,* which I find magical and have heard more clearly in these times. Now I'm in Quito, but I spent time in Peguche (my community), where I walked with my brothers in the forest of the waterfall, to greet it and ask for energy. The animals went out into the space that was theirs, although temporarily. *Samay* is a word I often heard from my parents. It means the breath of life, or pulse – that is, everything.

YLLO

Inua Ellams & Omar Musa

Fuck / Batman

The promise was / should one fall into a cave of bats / should one be engulfed by hundreds of beating wings / should one be beaten / scratched or bitten / one would emerge / half-human half-invincible / enough to sharpen fear down to a tight-toothed weapon / with which to gnaw the criminal urban underworld / down to pulpy nothings / protecting us all / The promise was / should an animal's essence seep into a child / knowing what damage loose power brews / he would accept himself as host / his body a fleshy petri dish / to guide its mutation to goodness / Instead the promise / turned ravenous / leapt from host to host / country to country / blood to blood / its million teeth chewing through our simple lungs / We closed down our offices / it hung on our clothes / We fled from cities / it clung to our cars / We stayed in bed / it came for our dreams / a curdled crown / a rank coronation / a crude corroding of our inner sanctums / our public spaces / our minute planning / our mapped-out futures / horoscopes and forecasts / the dark parts of star charts / all emptied out / to an assiduous stillness / the promise gorging on our numbed lives / our startled terror / And when the promise retreated / it left its fangs in the sky / its claws in our pockets / its foul breath huffed between us in shopping lines / its warning to return should we cease vigilance / to claim more from the survived

IE

Fuck \ Batman (Part 2)

The truth is parts of us welcomed \ the prophet of oblivion \ its thousand rapturous faces \ the flapping beat of its leathery wings \ its messianic cape \ like an accelerant of armageddon \ its balled-up breath plummeting down \ crumpling the traffic jams of our silent screaming \ a weight unknown \ we had always known \ The truth is parts of us secretly rejoiced \ that we could finally drop our masks \ relinquish the facade of civility \ and welcome the end days \ The wild children wore pasta necklaces \ hunted with sardine cans beaten into shanks \ and streamed toilet paper across the emptied cities \ The grandfathers listening to radio broadcasts \ sanitised their hands with night-brewed moonshine \ and came to different conclusions \ The grandmothers grew parsley and shot Zoom bombers \ There were voices swooping in the skies above the streets \ We sat on our windowsills and drank ink \ singing lockdown nocturnes \ cabin fever-dreaming \ unscrambling our future from a mess of blinding stars \ We looked for patterns and rearranged history \ We made jigsaw pictures of places we might never visit again \ There is Mount Kinabalu and the Tamparuli Bridge \ Here is Semporna with yellow and pink coral \ There are the reefs that will breath again \ Here are turtles and their quiet hymns \ We grew madder yet clearer-headed with each day \ We cried and laughed and cried again \ We chiselled our faces to suit our moods \ and settled on perverse Joker smiles \ We melted all the votive candles we had lit in tribute to our pasts \ and recast them as clear crayons \ to create the myths of our tomorrows

OM

COLLABORATION STATEMENT
Inua Ellams & Omar Musa

Omar Musa is a friend and fellow poet and writer. We met in Australia a few years ago when I was artist in residence of the Perth International Arts Festival. When I began working on my poem for the anthology, I wanted to bridge the space between fantasy and reality; between what we knew of the origins of Covid-19, and what might have been had it begun in another dimension. I thought then of Omar, who lived in an almost polar opposite part of the world to me, and wondered then how his poetics and imagination, both in literary and visual capacities might compliment or contrast mine.

IE

With both the images and the words, I wanted to create a phantasmagoria that represents the absurdity of our lives at the moment. I hoped that by combining pop culture references, images from the natural world (in particular, my homeland Borneo) and hints at religiosity, it would create a sense of unease and longing. Working with Inua was an honour – together I think we were able to sculpt these feverdreams of our days and times into something I'm really proud of.

OM

Matthew Welton
&
Hazel Smith

HOLDING THE VERTICAL

I'm not cycling home across the park and up the ring road as the drivers wind down their windows and two kinds of hip-hop drift into the afternoon.

I'm not bussing to the gym, swapping pleasantries with the girl on the door, donning headphones while lifting weights, befuddled by gaps in the storyline because I forgot to listen.

I'm not showing up early to the coffee place so I can get a seat at the long wooden table.

I'm not dining out, attacking a tangy Thai salad while chatting to the restaurant owner who bemoans the sky-high rents, then serves up an 'on-the-house' crème caramel to share for our dessert.

I'm not pitching up in the field for family camping, then heading over to the Folk Tent to check out the bands.

I'm not traveling twenty-four hours to an overcast dawn in London, gobbling bagels then fretting about calories, blackberrying with my nieces until we are all purple-lipped, basking in The Proms while blasting the acoustics.

Some days my walk takes me round the cemetery on the hill where the grass has grown over the footpaths and the headstones are still just readable, and often there's a robin on the high brick wall.

Sometimes we amble on the beach below our house, yachts stochastic in the bay, sky clenched blue. Sometimes we cut across the peninsula to where the ocean waves let loose and marvel when surfers hold the vertical.

I haven't mentioned the baby yet: our baby was four months old before we could let my mother hold him.

I have been wanting to talk about the gallery installation I've been working on with an artist-friend: it remixes our childhoods through two doppelgängers, behind whom we can comfortably collide. We exhibit next month but we can't have a launch or headphones for the video, and many who might normally have come to it won't.

If I'd been listening to this much Bandcamp without making recommendations there'd have to be something seriously up, so: Food People, Doomshakalaka, Paul Carbuncle, Matt Hill, Burnt Paw, Corey Mwamba, Kirsty McGee. How about you let me know what you think?

We have different listening trajectories, but we are in this sonically together, writing down what we are hearing, grabbing language by the ear, listening to each other listening. And thank you for being such an A1 recommender system, shifting me noiselessly from Corey to Kirsty, from vibraphone to voice. You are a lot smarter than Amazon, which usually recommends me my own books.

Nobody is stopping me and asking for directions. I'm getting better at shopping lists. I couldn't tell you when I last heard the doorbell and wondered who was there.

I'm socialising on Skype without the effort of 'entertaining'. I'm peeping at virtual film festivals around the world. I'm growing my hair long for the first time in decades. I'm relieved not to be publicly performing, to play instead the hermetic role of introvert. And I am pushing towards the out-of-reach while day-dreaming — curiously relaxed, mug in hand — at my home desk.

I'm cutting down on beer, but making coffee more often. The kitchen radio never turns off. The moths got at my sweaters. The baby's getting teeth. I don't know where I put my dictionary. I'm photographing the walls.

Wishing that people in Sydney would wear masks. Wishing they would keep to their side of the pavement. Wishing they would retain a modicum of fear, shed this bravado of the normal. On the ferry from Cronulla to Bundeena everyone crammed together and without even a gesture towards face-covering. A seat in the corner, sanitised by blasts of fresh air as the door swings open and children run out onto the deck.

I seem to be talking to myself more than ever and, when I'm queueing in the supermarket or wandering across the park, I notice my voice getting breathier and sometimes mildly tetchy.

Every day I search online for the latest figures in New South Wales which are usually very low. But the statistics seem permanently giddy and can rise as quickly as they fall. Then there's the media mantra about undetected transmission, nudging fear of the unknown. Vigilance versus paranoia, certainty versus risk. Some friends cannot abide video calls and will not thrive on neglect. Intimacy and distance, she said, that's the paradox the virus dictates.

Some days I come home from my walk not really sure of where I've been, but knowing precisely how the wind has ruffled the branches, or blown the litter from the bins or made my thoughts feel irretrievable.

Sometimes my happiness seems perverse, even shameful, a state of mind it is embarrassing to disclose. Often restrictions have been freeing, restoring a previously snatched balance. Frequently I immerse myself in BBC World or surf The Guardian on my iPad. Then I wonder if my hyper-cautiousness is actually anxiety transfer from hard-hit Britain to hardly-hit Australia.

We make what we can of whatever is to hand and that, I guess, is a world: boats in a bay, an overcast dawn, blackberries, wooden tables, a robin on a wall.

A streak of taking turns, of turnabouts, of turntables. The shake of the vicarious: a newborn child, the joy of family camping. The world sectioned like an apple, albeit a diseased one; a stranger made less strange. Intimacy and distance my friend said, that's how it all pans out. And with those words, listening turned into writing, solipsism into exchanges, surrogates into experiences.

COLLABORATION STATEMENT
Matthew Welton & Hazel Smith

We met when we gave a poetry reading together in 2018 at Five Leaves Bookshop in Nottingham but were already familiar with some aspects of each other's work. We decided to take short turns in writing using email as our medium. Since we share a mutual admiration for Frank O'Hara's poetry, Matt suggested we start with an 'I do this, I do that' approach though in the negative, that is stressing what we were *not* doing during the pandemic. This was a useful starting point and resulted in a 'call and response' mode of working which is reflected in the systematic alternation of voices. After that the collaboration built its own momentum and went through various stylistic changes including directly addressing each other and becoming a little more reflective and abstracted towards the end: it appears here in the order in which it was written. We both remarked that our approach in the collaboration was more autobiographical than is normal for us. We also found that the differences between the experience of the pandemic in the UK and Australia emerged as the collaboration progressed.

Vidyan Ravinthiran
&
Arvind Krishna Mehrotra

LOVE IN THE TIME OF COVID

In condos on full moon nights,
standing on balconies,
they blow conch shells

and wave tricolours
to scare off the animals
come home from the wild

to reclaim the land where jackals sang
when you were a girl.
Look out the window. There's one singing.

from LAKESIDE WALKS

A poem like a tree
can be dated precisely.

For instance today
I saw a blue
face mask hanging
on a branch.

from Lockdown Garden

Close to each other,
socially undistanced,
the mulberry leaves,

uniformly green,
shall turn brown together.
It's like a herd dying.

    *

In the heap of dead
leaves crinkly as
brown skins, those
breathing things
foraging around
the bamboo stand
are jungle babblers.

    *

It was planted
all wrong, too
close to a wall,
under the mango
trees. There was
nowhere for it
to go except up
like a mast and
that's where
it went, taking
its leaves with it –
long, tapering.
I never saw them
fall. It never
flowered, which
would've helped
me look it up in a

book of flowering
Indian trees. Now
I'll never know
its name nor of
the bird singing
at evening
in the shrubbery.

*

She stood outside
the gate, a woman
my age, head covered
with flowery print,
a sickle in her hand.

Could she come
inside and cut
grass for her goats?
It was ankle high.
Her face was inches

from mine and I felt
her breath on my skin.
It's after I'd turned
the corner that I heard
what she'd said.

*

The shingles unwalked on,
the doors bolted,
the squirrels back in their nests.

Under the moon a bird floats
and settles on a branch.
The sky is pale.

The leaves of the ironwood
when new every spring
are a deep pink.

The evening goes out like a flame.
We've seen different things.
It's always been so.

Tell me, love, what you saw today.

    *

The garden, unlike you, is
a daytime presence. I wait

for this night to be over,
for the trees to reappear
in window and doorway.

    *

The milk thistle's
bud I saw in
the pink of health

is a white smudge,
like a child's drawing
rubbed with spittle.

    *

As I came up with the morning papers,
the pigeon walking on the balustrade
flew off to join two squirrels

under the plumeria,
leaving me alone to read the day's headlines
which I knew from the day before.

    *

Around this time every evening
I'm out in the garden, looking for things to pick.
The drumstick has again lost half its height
and the dilennia's fast losing its leaves.
The ironwood is white with flowers.
Yesterday something petal-like was
lying near it when I came in. It was getting
dark. It's getting dark now too.
The dilennia's leafless, the ironwood's flowering,
and my basket's heavy with leaves, petals, and dusk.

*

The day is joyous.
Green string lights on trees.
Each leaf's covered
and no leaf's fused.

There's a Zoom wedding on
and you're in bridal dress.
Its flight reflected in a puddle,
a bird passes overhead.

Those banyans

at Muthur are murder
to write about – how to seize on such
thew and sinew, melding and widening?
– "Going viral," I want to say, an idiom we must retire…

Roots in the air and soil both
– like me, like you; the wire, the idea of a wire,
akin to leaves a chisel planted
aforetime in a Gothic cathedral, belongs to nature.

The economist's dream of perpetual growth.
Your paki shop, become a chain. That tree
with a hole in it like a ripped-out hearth;

soldiers did that, it was Pillayar's shrine
but the god-figure was nicked from his nook
but on either side, his pillars live on and on.

SRI LANKA

is every country
where I feel, and don't feel, at home

– a child,
leaving England the first time
for Colombo's eerily
warm evenings and the alien
language of crickets,

I too was
fostered alike by beauty and by fear.

For many a year
through the doorway of dusk
I'd travel there.

"What's wrong?" someone might say
or, "I love to see you smile";
but I was far away.

*

In lockdown with my wife and baby
in green Acton's
twilit warmth

I'm that lonely boy
listening for crickets
on a pink-tiled rooftop in Dehiwala.

*

What of this country
where I live now but should I leave
– if, say, the virus

touches my parents in England –
my visa may bar our return? Out
of caves in our garden's stone

wall peeps the immortal
squirrel I saw run
through ancient Polonnaruwa,

three white lines
burned into its back:
the fingermarks of Rama.

The comedian

's
stylized
incredulity

concerning
politics

is something to watch

COLLABORATION STATEMENT
Arvind Krishna Mehrotra & Vidyan Ravinthiran

My Sri Lankan family likes to consider video-calling a means of actually being together: at one point, my cousins in Nova Scotia and Sydney phoned my uncle in Colombo daily, leaving the camera running as they went about their business. As if their distant sitting rooms shared an ocean-crossing window or tunnel, magically connecting their lives and reversing the traumas that have scattered Tamils across the world.

The magic trick doesn't work for me. Having moved to the US with a young baby, I've felt acutely the restrictions on travel: Frank's grandparents haven't held him in nearly a year, and whether he recognizes them on Skype isn't clear. Nor is it clear that if I did fly back from the US to the UK, my visa would let me return. I've found myself writing poems directly out of this experience of separation amounting to entrapment. But I also, in a strange new country, with different weather and flora and fauna, thought back to, or more helplessly reinhabited, my childhood visits to Sri Lanka. Sometimes I feel distant from where I'd like to be. At other times it feels a sort of no-place where memories grow newly pungent.

VR

The sense of smell, they say, is a warning sign. If you lose it, you should be worried. It may mean that you have Covid-19. I who never went near a flower in order to know its smell, now poke my nose into every bee-laden bush. I also notice the weeds in the garden, more than I ever did. Some of the weeds have flowers tiny as pinpricks. I have to go down on my knees to confirm that what I am seeing is not a speck. As lockdown days become weeks, then months, and I learn the names of the plants, a dead garden comes alive with words: milk thistle, bloodleaves, hophead Philippine violet, king's mantle, rain lily, arrowhead vine. Little read books are pulled out of shelves greedily. Opening Molly Mahood's *A John Clare Flora*, I find mentioned the Himalayan Balsam. I live in the Himalayan foothills, in Dehra Dun. The world is a small place. A flower bed could have contained it.

AKM

Anthony Caleshu
&
Mariko Nagai

Lockdown in the Sound

I was swimming
when the lockdown started
and was now thoroughly lost.

     The lockdown started
     and I swam in the lost.

The tritium, once leaked
into the Sound,
now sounded like bees.

     Triton lives in the Sound
     lost for so many years:
     as children are lost, he is lost.

I swam in the sound
of nuclear subs,
wrist-watch illuminating
the fauna.

     The subsonic sound of
     the leak from the Sound
     illuminated fins underwater.

For 30 years the subs haven't leaked
tritium, but now bloom trillium during this
lockdown: the three white flowers rising
up like the seaweed beneath.

> The flowers bloom like
> leaked rheum from ileum.
> Did I tell you that tumors
> have blossomed out of
> season inside of my
> mother? No radiation
> helps. She leaks. She
> sheds. The body has
> locked down.

The wifi signal is weak
underwater, our Zoom incomplete.

> We live in the past,
> the present, the future.

Blown out to sea, we moor
our bodies to a lobster pot.

> Each year is imprinted on
> a lobster's body. They
> are not witnesses to what
> the land suffers but they
> sense the changes in the
> water.

Lobsters like dogs
communicate by urine.

> One limb at a time, I crawl
> through the sea, out of
> the sea, onto the land.

In the stories, our elegies
for others are always
the elegies for ourselves.

> And the funeral, not for
> the dead but us, the
> dying.

Everything is in motion,
perpetuating – but our Zoom
is not ambitious – the moon wanes.

                    During the lockdown, we
                    live through zooming into
                    aspects of our lives, lives
                    lived through the
                    microscope. We look
                    closely, and live closely,
                    so closely we've
                    forgotten how to live as a
                    whole.

In the distant future I am
swimming through the
murk of algae blooms
and viral loads.

                    In the distant
                    future, I am unloading
                    in the present tense and
                    the future perfect.

In the future perfect,
fish will have swum
for a long time with masks –

                    We take off our masks
                    when we swim, and we
                    know what it is we are
                    missing.

My mother, as she was
leaving, said, 'Will I see
you again? Will I come out alive?'

                    To my mother, as I was
                    leaving, I said, 'I am
                    going for a swim.'

So I went for a swim
in the Sound where Triton lived,
but I am a child,
and like all children, I am lost.

        In the future, I will find
        you, Mother, walking on
        water lilies.

But for now, you sleep
in your watery grave,
tubes draining you
of the sea that's drowning you
from inside out.

        Our heart beats amplify
        in water, our heart beats are running
        through our bones.

In our bones, we can feel
another wave coming.

        In our bones, the
        language blows with the
        currents below.

We water the plants,
water our hearts, our
lungs, even our bones
in this Sound are watery.

COLLABORATION STATEMENT
Anthony Caleshu & Mariko Nagai

Anthony was introduced to Mariko via a mutual friend with whom he shares an interest in Japanese literature. In an early email, Mariko shared Brandon Shimoda's fascinating project, 'The Afterlife, Part 4: The Ancestors Reside in the Answers Themselves' (https://future-feed.net/the-afterlife-part-4-the-ancestors-reside-in-the-answers-themselves). The project served as a springboard, prompting us into the territory of sharing lockdown dreams, TV, encounters with the otherworldly, and family. With Anthony in Plymouth, England and Mariko in Tokyo, our collaboration began by asking questions about each other's geographies and how we were managing to experience the world amidst lockdown. Anthony's regular swims in the Plymouth Sound set the stage for a poem, which would range through both of our real and imagined new world orders, from metaphors around what it meant to be lost, to Mariko's mother slowly losing control of her body from Stage 4 cancer. Over the summer months, we traded long lines via nearly daily emails – lines which moved in and out of voices and language-play, and which became projected short stanzas during our short revision process in late October.

Selima Hill
&
Wang Xiaoni
(*translated by Eleanor Goodman*)

How to Float

Nothing else matters to me now,
nothing except food
and how to float
and how to take no notice of the clocks,
and how to reinvent myself as somebody
who's not so much a person
as a turtle
who bobs along
doing nothing much,
a turtle whose idea of bliss is mud,
mud, sludge, anything pointless,
and do I miss the ticking?
I do not.

SH

By the Window

Sometimes, you can only be like a person.
The plates filled with food are not yet on the table
the bees and butterflies come
bringing their inscribed wings.
Aside from a person, what else can you be—
the turtle going off to sing in the grass says
you could never pass yourself off as him.
The autumn sun
keeps roasting the book's printed spine
I've stood by this window for too long
even the bent shadows seem so much like a person.

WX

February, Father and Son Carrying Packages in the Rain

The father is carrying
hard alcohol or beer in his arms
the child is carrying hard alcohol or juice
either way, what is oscillating is liquid.
Both father and son have damp hair
the child can be no older than three
he's still so small
he hasn't had time to understand.
But the father,
why is he clutching onto anything that isn't his child,
why isn't he holding tight to
that shimmering body.
The rain falls, neither heavy nor light
wetting the upper half of the faces people reveal
stricken with grief.

Note 1: This poem is part of a series called "Isolation"
Note 2: In the first part of this year, because of the pandemic, residents who ordered items online had to leave their residential compounds to pick up the items themselves at designated locations.

WX

The Picnic

It's good to feel sand between your toes,
to feel salty kisses on your cheek,

to watch the gulls wheeling overhead,
to race bare-chested out across the beach;

and now the father runs into the sea
and dives into the beautiful white waves,

the little boy runs off towards his mother,
his tiny body glittering with sand;

they're opening an enormous yellow bag
and spreading out a picnic on the rug;

it's good to feel nourished by patience,
it's good to be reminded how to hope.

SH

Original Poems by Wang Xiaoni

窗前

有时候还只能像人。
盛食物的平盘还没上桌
蜜蜂和蝴蝶来了
自带镂花的翅膀。
除了像人还能像什么
要去草丛唱歌的乌龟说
冒充它可不行。
秋天的阳光
再三烤着印了字的书脊
在这幅窗前站得太久
连弯下去的阴影也太像个人了。

二月，雨里抱快递的父子

那父亲怀里
抱的是酒精还是酒
那孩子抱的是酒精还是果汁
晃晃荡荡的不过一些液体。
父子俩头发都湿了
估计那孩子只有三岁
他还那么小
什么都来不及懂。
可是，那父亲
为什么他紧抱的不是他的孩子
他的上身为什么
不是紧贴那团水灵灵的肉。
雨不大不小
淋着所有人露出来的上半张脸
看着特别特别伤心。

注释1：这是组诗《隔离》中的一首
注释2：今年早些时候，网络购买物品要由住户自行去社区外的指定地点领取。

COLLABORATION STATEMENT
Wang Xiaoni & Selima Hill

When Eleanor sent me her Chinese translation of Selima's poem "How to Float", the lines that moved me the most were: "and how to reinvent myself as somebody / who's not so much a person / as a turtle". Indeed, in this time of endless crisis, we all feel a little less human. On a deeper or more mysterious level, however, all of the myriad things that happen to us each day on earth, without exception, is part of being human. One must admit that "person" is a complex word, one that encompasses disappointment and grief, and that was the inspiration behind my poem "By the Window".

WX

In a time of terrible suffering and fear, one often feels an equally terrifying sense of helplessness. Serving as a translator for this project gave me a pleasant sense of purpose, albeit within a small scope. But that small scope is, I believe, of essential importance to what makes us human. Turtles perhaps have their own poems, but the only poetry truly known to us is our own – and what would we be without it?

EG

Collaborating with other artists is definitely the most fun part of my life as a poet, in spite of, or perhaps because of, it being the most challenging. I love the sense of fellowship it brings. Often I feel self-indulgent as a poet, and pointless; working together for the sake of our shared planet feels so good. Perhaps that is why I don't have a car, computer, mobile phone, TV, or cooker. It feels more respectful and more intimate. I can sit quietly at home and feel close to a stranger, to Wang Xiaoni, a fellow poet, sitting in her own home, far away in China, where I have never been. My aim was to write simply; to counter Wang Xiaoni's *grief* with *hope* and *gratitude*; to respond, in particular, to Wang Xiaoni's moving image of the son's shimmering body.

SH

Declan Ryan
&
Linda Stern Zisquit

My Guide, My Surprise

Dear Dario,

I've been held *captive*
by an obsessive love, *kept
within bounds, controlled,
confined, captivated, charmed.*
It took these five months at home

to loosen the hold.
"I have sat and listened to
too many words of
the collaborating muse…"
and plot too freely with life.

Franca, Dear

helpless as Racine,
you lance through profound places;
ever snaking inward,
a whipstock, Roman candle,
can I dare call you *Sister*?

My guide, my surprise,
when my poor mind was troubled
you made for my body;
your spring parts and unites,
fish who cuts your nets and chains.

Dario,

I'm not managing
to concentrate. Let alone
collaborate. Now
August already! Dolphin,
eel, Sargasso Sea retreat

into distances.
We'll inspire each other.
Your comic faces,
my indulgence, your skittish
rebellions, and my grounding.

Not Rodin's Camille
who sculpted his hands and feet
to leave center stage
and be committed insane,
I'm here to stay, in orbit.

Here is my hand please take it.
Amulet, surprise,
peonies tightly fragrant.
Let the ants devour the sticky
film and open desire.

Let the month go by
slowly. I'll gather its fruit
and reel in our line
with its sensuous fishes
wobbling again in my mind

Dear Camille,

the month has got away
as in a dream: the ants march
along its dull spotlight;
the wobble in the mind,
or I dream like patchwork Daniel:

Rodin's feet are clay
like all golden headed idols',
his hand, his living hand,
it reaches out to yours;
nightingale in flight, now land.

My brother,

Tomorrow I'll hew
again. Like a prayer between
sobs. We plumb the depths
to come back into the world—
informed as much by good as

errors of the past.
You do not want to get lost,
he said. But I did!
Oh, how I loved the bliss of
indecision, flights and dreams!

"This work of transformed
and distorted memory—"
If we circle back
was the writing on the wall?
Was there a plan all along?

Sister, Franca,

I see you surface:
you escaped your death struggle
with your life; the bliss
of never being born is lost,
you knock yourself out

to be like everyone.
Sob your prayers to the master
of the snowflake, circle

back – the past is never past.
I swore never to care

after so many deaths,
I cry on my own shoulder,
Sargasso Sea retreat:
one plot, the same old always plot,
the spotlight stage deserted.

To D—

It was a turn from
hurt. And self-absorption. Our
extraordinary
complicity! *I am no
longer what I have made of*

*myself but what we
have made of me.* Losing is
the only way to
empty and make room, hope of
more to come ripe in the wound.

But I'm back! How could
I leave without an encore?
"Summer like a bee
sucks out our best." Plague persists.
Yet we prepare the earth for spring.

COLLABORATION STATEMENT
Declan Ryan & Linda Stern Zisquit

Collaborate? We'd met once at our mutual book launch last May. Appreciated each other's work. But put our heads together? During the year we had started corresponding, I'd read a few of Dec's excellent reviews and wrote to tell him how moved I was. His responses had been warm, thoughtful. But collaborate? Dec suggested we use the letter-form. At the time I was reading the *Dolphin Letters* and Lowell's *Dolphin*. Lowell was a poet I'd never given much attention, always Elizabeth Bishop had eclipsed him. But something changed during these months. I suggested we use the Japanese Tanka form, five lines, syllabics of 5-7-5-7-7. Collaborators Dario Fo and Franca Rame were our initial personae. Lowell, Hardwick, Montale, Clivia entered. And Camille Claudel and Rodin, the Biblical Daniel, and later Camus and Maria Casares. And Berryman. And our own lives with their various pulls and pains. It was uncanny how whatever one of us wrote it would touch exactly where the other was in mind or heart or study. It's been inspiring, stimulating, fun, life-giving, energizing. And it brought us close. For which I am deeply grateful.

LSZ

As Linda says, we'd been in touch after our pamphlet launch, admiringly, and had started corresponding a little about shared writers – Lawrence Joseph, James Salter, an essay on Dario Fo. The collaboration came at a great time – I've loved how we were able to veer around among what we had been reading separately and how often that coincided anyway; Hardwick's prose, Lowell's letters – we both have a fondness for that form, and for the magpie-ing instinct of taking a line or two as a starting point or spur from what we've been reading, as a way of thinking our way in. The letter-form made it all feel very companionable, it was good to have such company in the great shut-down. Funny how often even when we were lurching around between enthusiasms it hit a point the other had got to in the mean-time. What fun.

DR

David Herd
&
Sharmistha Mohanty

Like the world not yet

The little girl is lost, to others. She knows where she is, protected by the mountains behind her and the sea ahead, the natural barriers of the sub-continent. She lives on the plains in between, in the forests and by the rivers. Sometimes, when she stands on one leg while playing, she can feel the land moving, in its almost imperceptible tectonic travel northeast. She knows she is not alone. A wind from another geologic age moves through the forests, inconsolable, it creates waves on the rivers. The little girl is embryonic, like the world not yet created from the vast, dark waters at the beginning of time. She contains lives within her but it is as a little child that she remains most potent, most potential. Her grown self comes to visit her often, holding the child in her lap, feeling her unblemished skin. The child wraps her arms around the neck of her older self. They look at each other. The little girl is already able to withstand. But she can also break, because breaking is an ability. She knows what her older self forgets, that they are both capable of crossing their own finitude. Others have lost the little girl in their centrifugal dispersion. But she, travelling in the opposite direction, can see everything, the sorrow that comes from the impermanence of things, the depths of the ordinary, the sweep of the river valleys and the way her solitude alternately lights up and darkens the landscape.

[SM]

*

A couple hold each other's hands against a northern landscape. They are not lost but each day they walk as if recovering their ground, the earth where they would stand and where the sky shapes towards their horizon in the patterns against the tree line where against the evening they remember stars. One by one. And they know that they have come this way before, as children to whom the world seemed open and immense, and they would gather what they could find albeit under the cover of childhood, or after, as they followed toward their younger selves. As if the sequence would carry on. They had been bearers of this conviction. Now they step out each September evening as if discovering their way, across the valleys and the fields as if they might co-ordinate their motion, to the scale of the understanding the new beginning brings. This is the dance. It feels to them like a slow waltz. As the chords with which they are familiar fall away. They are left to find their step and on the hard earth, as they witness and where the distances are not the same. And they try to listen for the sounds, name what they hear calling, articulate the rhythms of that which is coming to pass. They walk and as they walk they mark the old bearings, the ordinary as it falters, the new dance.

[DH]

*

A tapir moves on the banks of the Las Piedras river in the Amazon forest. Behind him, the banks rise into low, green cliffs dense with vegetation and trees. The tapir moves very slowly, looking down at the ground, prehistoric animal, walking with the weight of the millions of years that his species has been here, with each step moving from his origins till today.
Mourn the sight dimmed from sewing up the near, the lost measure of the near and the far, mourn the indivisible individual, the assertions that lash the air, mourn the end of what can be attained only by asking, the time when deep was the depth, mourn the fatal arrhythmia at the heart of things, the faltering of wings and eyelids and hands and breath.

[SM]

*

If they could dance they would dance but the air falters. They wish they could talk about the moment when the world lost its breath, how it felt to be on the earth while the snows melted, how they had crossed over, started to count what was left. The things they could do without. That which they couldn't learn not to live with. Leaving. Or maybe the feeling that they were coming back, having spoken and made plans, and knowing all they planned might not yet happen, but it wouldn't matter because something surely would come to pass. Something they might think of as an event and one by one they would re-make the narrative. How things started before there were imaginations in the astral dark and how the snows came and the rain and each day had its own adventure and they would sleep and in the morning they would resume their part. Of living and looking out. They knew that they had come this way before. But never in a season when the world had stopped. Futures fallen away and in the dark the breathless, fighting against the element until the light dropped. Until the loved ones had gone. Until the days had righted. Until the tapir and the humans had crossed the earth. As they wished and as they spoke. As if it was the moment after. Not the dance that was coming. So still they walked.

[DH]

*

The air falters and the measure of making, of doing, is undone. To make is to work always against the unmade, looking far, seeing what is not yet. Behind what is there are dying herbs and seeds, languages lying in the undergrowth, beliefs in the deep riverbeds, ways of knowing, of being, decomposing in the soil. The world grows narrower, thinner. Forests are felled and brushed back from the highways, no dirt or mud anywhere. The two lines of the road will meet, exactly as the law of perspective says, at infinity.

[SM]

*

They walk. This is undone business they have before them. They are learning quickly what they wanted to protect. Like the passage of events, how the world would just have kept on happening, at street corners accidentally running into friends. Or people you hardly knew, those with whole lifetimes of stories, who would tell you one and that way the day would be spent, quietly, not in style, like people happened to be connecting, intending seriously they should do this again. Talking and splitting off. Carrying part of the others with them. Like the girl in the mountains who laid down her thread, so that she knew, if she needed, this was a place she might come back to, sleep, somewhere she would catch her breath. Listen. Take a breath. The couple didn't know what it would come to. But each evening as the dark came they tried to find their step. Stars against the trees and the hard earth stretched before them. Remembered futures. Days left.

[DH]

COLLABORATION STATEMENT
Sharmistha Mohanty & David Herd

Difference, as between the elements – earth, water, air – that combine to form new things, difference as the most elemental condition. The world, even under the pandemic, is not *global*. It only seems so from the centres of "power". Geographies still express themselves through their own sounds, their own rituals, their own particular needs.

We wrote in dialogue, one after the other, each trying to recover their bearings in the world. We wanted to acknowledge, as we wrote, that we didn't know what was coming next. We wanted the uncertainty to be our conversation's condition.

We came from what and where we were. The bells of Canterbury which sounded each evening to mark the deaths, the silenced street cries of Mumbai, without any effort to build ideas, rather to listen to each other.

It was if we were exchanging letters, with the altered sounds of our environments in our ears, and with the other's words playing through our imaginations. Our settings have been changed and we wanted to share what that change meant. And between us we wanted to understand what might now be different.

Luke Kennard
&
Hwang Yu Won
(*translated by Jake Levine*)

Entirely Wrong
(and the Sky is Made of Gold)

Eternal interregnum, organic anacoluthon.
Dented apologia, the syncretic dogs.
Did everyone have their little book, yes?
Wanted to be the one to point it out,
minor variation, cruel impasto, comic arpeggio.
I felt sad in the toyshop with no children in it,
the way the clown, the way you must resign,
you must resign clown your position
has become untenable, blackballed, ask for a chair
prior to this: world overseen by god or even humanism,
how we divide the world, waste an aesthetic act;
someone will receive it but they will not understand
for the song to be interrupted, for the song interrupts
itself. It's worse than that with electricity.
How much would that sandwich counter set you back?
I ask because I am obsessed with money.
Machine for the improvement of all musical
performance, machine, the will of somebody
learning to die well, tempo rubato, baby
and I know it, thumbs through worn booklet
thumbs nose, *you become trapped in the order
you create*, right? Trying to be so thorough,
so honest, the stammer is the important bit:
right now there is very little left to predict.

The Meditating Buddha Sitting Full-Lotus that Meditates on the Beginning of Winter

I am still here, sitting with my head in my hands
and over there on top of that table
if the vases are really trembl-ling
their trembling is a trembling that is really only me—

Only me
in a way
where the trembling won't stop

until it becomes the trembling of the entire world.

On the cold special floor that is found in only Korean buildings,
in the time it takes
for the autumnal grass hanging upside down on the wall to dry,
the left sole of the foot of the Meditating Buddha Sitting Full-Lotus
turns white as rice.

Hanging outside the window, floating in the sky
is a water scooping pot.
Shaky, shaky,
splashy, splash and

within the widening surface
of the wings that spill from the
acute and light emitting
spreading out of the
shattering of the water pot

is a cold that grows
from foot to knee
through pelvis to chest
until finally coming
to brainfreeze at the head.

What's so fucking special about a Buddha sitting full-lotus anyway?
It's not even as nice as a handful of cool wind,
or ten minutes of wide-open ventilation.

Like pounding the enter key, I jump up!
Intending to dash to the window, I hesitate
like pressing Spacebar like
Space,
and then
Space,
I remove my sleeping
feet.

What's so special about the Standing, Gold-Plated Buddha anyway?
Whenever the sky turns sky-colored for the first time in who remembers when,
anyone that stands in front of an open window can momentarily expand.

Yes, the face is a thing like a runway –
between expressions that fly without permission overhead
and the familiar ones that frequently land,
the corners of the Standing, Gold-Plated Buddha's mouth
always end in an expression that takes off
and never comes back.
The meditation of the Meditating Buddha Sitting Full-Lotus
becomes white and

the only difference between Gold-Plated Future Buddha sitting in meditation
and Standing, Gold-Plated Buddha
is just a serial number.

I press Spacebar.
I pound Enter.
If it were possible to do this in reverse,
wouldn't that be a surprise?

Because when it does happen in reverse
the fire of the candles collapse into the night sea and
the becoming of the sea of flames is made up of
horizontal lines, vertical lines,
border lines, etc…
until it is that which is every line.

And if that fire caught on to the night wind, if that fire swelled,
no, no, don't even think it.
It would be bad.
Yeah, it would be bad, but
bad does not mean impossible.

Because every time that happens, Brake, Brake,
in the distance, the smell of burning tires on a road near the beach.
The way water expands,
an overflowing season of flames.

Waterfire, firewater, with no discrimination,
in this late Fall when I finger the untouchable clouds
for a long time with eyes that don't even have fingers,
on the morning of the final day,

for the duration of time I hold down the spacebar,
the meditation of the Meditating Buddha Sitting Full-Lotus
spills into the sky.

Standing, Gold-Plated Buddha, whatever,
Enter,
Enter,
flop there, crash down,
collapse.

COLLABORATION STATEMENT
Luke Kennard & Hwang Yu Won

I first worked with Yu Won in 2017 in an exchange as part of Steven Fowler's Enemies project, which involved a collaborative performance of new work in London and Seoul. At the time, while we were preparing, he said, "The only, and maybe the biggest problem, seems like the fact that we use totally different languages." In the event, the biggest problem was that, while Yu Won was in fact fluent in English, I had no other language whatsoever. We decided to work with existing poems by Yu Won, into which I would write interjections, notes and reactions. For this *Poetry and Covid* project, there was time to write, but not necessarily time to translate, edit and react to the translations. We took a similar approach – a poem by Yu Won which had been written and translated during the first lockdown, which I was able to respond to. I've often talked to my students about using the things we believe to be holding us back as the material for our work, and maybe that pollyanna-ish advice was on my mind as I wrote this poem in the midst of a kind of brain fog, trying to notice the things which were making me feel flat or sad or uninspired or just as though there was no point in trying to express it. Yu Won's work, I believe, has a more straightforwardly wise and insightful perspective; the medicine rather than the list of side-effects.

André Naffis-Sahely
&
Stacy Hardy

The Bond
for Stacy Hardy

The dry August air reeks of wood and ash
and the smoke plumes
leaving the rocky bowl of the San Gabriels
sink to kiss the lawn.

The dogs bark themselves hoarse, their frightened
black throats as charred
as the wounded hillsides. No refuge for coyotes,
raccoons, or the striped skunk,

as they scatter like sparks from a camper's hearth.
What is power if not
the ability to dislodge the living from
their synchronous groove?

After six months of death and disease, the rabbits
stir from their nests
in the crevices of rusty engines and people finally
begin to mourn.

On Verdugo, a cardboard placard stapled to
a half-stripped tree,
reads: 'Goodbye, Emilio', or, as the newspapers
called him, John Doe #283,

but nobody's heart's large enough to hold all the names
of the fallen. On either
side of the boulevard, a slew
of recession-raptured businesses:

'to let', 'for lease', 'pray for us' – and even the sign
above the gun-store,
ARMED & DANGEROUS says
'we're through'.

Today, my distant friend, I've only room for questions.
What does endurance mean
if it appears to be endless, what is grass if not gunpowder,
what is this chain of encampments

and shanties hugging the freeway if not humanity's take
on the Great Barrier Reef,
each person a polyp on the coral of concrete?
I think of you in Cairo

and your imprisoned comrades, another tinderbox
awaiting the flint-stone
of hurt… It is late at night,
so let every word

draw blood: everything is not going to be all right.
All my life, an unbroken
string of departures, a litany of leaving, but here
and there, faint glimmers

of meaningful connections, including you, my sister
from another mother,
another father, another world. Perhaps we shall soon
meet again, perhaps not,

perhaps the flowers stuffed into the beaked masks
of plague doctors provided
more comfort than safety, perhaps not,
but what gives us solace

between our first lungful of air and the last handful
of lime? The bond,
only the bond. So, where to now,
wanderer of the wastelands?

Drafts of Letters to A.
(September 1979–December 2020)
after Léona & André & for Aimé & Suzanne

I come from a deflowered country
devil thorns & flaming lilies.
Fever trees that weep bark
on skin knees.
I don't know what a marigold looks like.
Nor thrift nor columbine.
Is the collective noun an arrangement
or a massacre?
The peony, is she a flower?
Can she speak English?
Even the roses here are bitter,
petals curl against the sun.
Poppies, absurd eyeless infants.
They resemble only blind faces,
opium addicted fronds of flesh & bone.
Petals. Flowers. Beautiful precariousness,
starvation, banishment.

Here the rabbits
grow docile
under the blazing sun.
Mimic rocks piled
like a grave
on the hillside.
Even the dogs,
are godless.
Walking vertebrae
that slouch
through garbage.
Sixteen titties
like teeth, like bullets.
Below them,
the wrecks accumulate:
scrapyard,
broken concrete dreams,

& all those bodies
not exempt from gravity.

It's raining today,
& I'm just about to forget
how you spoke with your hands
the last day we met.

You were saying, disorientation occurs
if the spine bends too far backward.
We were in the Company Garden,
watching children learn to somersault.
It was hot
& you suggested
we sit: it means not twisting
to look at your own back.
But I was already
head over heels, bitterly
besotted & grass stained.
I tied my jersey around my waist
like in school & I had my period.
But still I felt it – we were sitting
at a distance
yet never so close.
Drinking the horror of summer,
of too many flowers, of blooming stillness
in the dead air, the redness of the soil
intermingled with our plasma;
You wanted to smoke a joint.
Don't –
I mumbled & stood up.
Stumbled
back to my cheap inner city rented apartment.

On my laptop,
I watch violence flower
on an animated map.
Like desertbloom
after a rainstorm.

6 townships, over 6 days.

Across the city
the displacement camps
are closing.
Shredded tarp flutters
carcass of a thousand tent homes
skinned to metal.
I saw a woman, lift
her hand, the same weight
as weeds, as the
dandelion stalks I offered.
I can't go home, she told me,
I'd rather kill myself, than die again.
Where would we go?
There is no safe place.
There is no electricity,
we are sitting in the dark.

Later she started to cry
& on a sudden impulse,
I too cried with her,
but our weeping
was lost in the echo –
tarp whipping tarp
a fricative rustling, as the wind mutinied,
& I strangled the last embraces of a derelict cigarette.

The streets are silent.
Dawn doesn't come,
it avoids blood spills.
The bakery
where I buy white bread
has closed down.
The men sit
& eat sunlight soap.
People are hungry;
are thirsty.
They stumble
full of curses.

Everyone speaks
through closed lips.

Last night, I fell asleep
checking my phone.
A salvation or carpus,
all my metacarpals
held in my right hand.
Woke up to the soft violence
of seeds, of remembrance.
The drooled dregs of
an unwritten poem
& my eyes
swollen with silences.

COLLABORATION STATEMENT
André Naffis-Sahely & Stacy Hardy

Our poems in this anthology are the fruit of our long fragmented friendship, having first met in Cape Town in 2014, and carried through our transitionings and traversings between Cairo, Limpopo, Makhanda, California and Pennsylvania in recent months, birthed out of the questions and thoughts prompted by this coronaviral moment, all lit by the initial spark of Stacy's suggestion that we play Suzanne and Aimé Césaire's 'Voice of the Oracle: A Surrealist Game', an exercise which helped bridge the distance between us as we attempted to reconnect and write poems dedicated to one another, for one another, which we hope will contain some worthwhile distillate of our conversations and shared connections.

Harriet Tarlo
&
Craig Santos Perez

Rain Sonnet During the Pandemic
November 1, 2020

Sunday morning rain. Church closed.
Our daughter wakes soaked
in urine. I give her a warm bath,
throw her sheets and dirty clothes
in the washing machine.
*The strongest typhoon of the year
is approaching the Philippines.*
Remember: rent is due today,
the election is Tuesday.
Our daughter's toes and fingers
wrinkle. The spin cycle begins. Lord,
please don't drown us
in the second wave of the virus
approaching the shore.

IF THE WEATHERS FIT
7 November 2020

Take heart, more than an
emoticon, shelter at home
away from the weight of
pins struck down & blasted
into stone. Tie favours to
the lintel, listen to invisible
oceans, dream of a cleaner
in a corner of the world who
could explain it all, open
rights of way again, sea
passages for invertebrates
quieten the kids, if the
weathers fit. Shoot, I've
lost all but the end of it.

Election Sonnet During the Pandemic
November 9, 2020

Past midnight, waiting, anxious news.
We voted for the "lesser evil," trusted
our ballots in the mail. Across the divided
nation, the counting continues—
why do we still have the electoral college?
Earlier today, my wife taught our daughter
the numbers song: "one, two, buckle
my shoe…" If they're killed in a car accident,
"three, four, open the door…" no president
would matter. "Five, six, pick up sticks…"
battleground states flip from red to blue.
"Seven, eight…" We turn off the tv, sigh
in darkness. "Lay them straight…" Covid
hospitalizations at an all-time high.

ALLEZ, ALLY ASTER
16 November 2020

Wind the bobbin up: a ring, a ring
of asters, star line above the mud
line around the water, direction
not widdershins, not counter to
season, purple rays paling into
autumn. A ring, a ring of hands un-
held, a separated standing round.
Still single figures, fishermen seen
across the reservoir, blue in gold
larch, green pine, then gone. Asters,
asters all fall down come winter,
always come up singing. Old rivers,
becks return in spate, old rhymes
permissions even: wind it back again.

COLLABORATION STATEMENT
Craig Santos Perez and Harriet Tarlo

We began from our very different places, but with a sense of being part of an all-too-joined up world, a world haunted by Climate Change and Covid-19. At the time CSP was writing sonnets. HT was writing 'Cut Flowers', a split form of her own that she found it hard to abandon. Both of us were busy juggling writing and teaching commitments with appearances and attendances on computer screens - these opening up our worlds yet further, whilst we remained at our homes due to the pandemic. We had never met. HT had approached CSP, taken by his *Unincorporated Territory* books, and having decided to teach his work to her M.A. students. We saw each other though, over the summer at the reading series for the More-than-Human-World ecopoetics anthology, an epic work about to come out with Spuyten Duyvil. There, in their little zoom frames, and their various time-frames, poets from all over the world shared diverse work around environment – fraught, fractured, joyous, holistic, sometimes despairing. The pandemic was sometimes talked about, often around the edges of the readings, in the discussions more than the works themselves. Somehow, we did not write toward the collaboration. But then, in the November, HT sent a rainy cut flower poem using found words from city dwellers about everything they felt cut off from. CSP replied with the first poem here. HT took up the challenge to inhabit a fourteen-line stanza, and the four poems came together. In response to the stresses evident in CSP's first poem, and having listened to recent interviews with him regarding the state of the ocean around the Pacific Islands, HT's first poem starts as a direct response but moves into a dream sequence of fantasy, hope, then sudden retreat from connection. CSP's next poem focusing on the American election that dominated November 2020 set off an exchange of children's rhymes between the two of us, rhymes which connect to deeper folk traditions of the past, as well as how place has changed. Both touch on separation, distance and loss.

Jennifer Cooke
&
Jèssica Pujol Duran

FLOORPLANS

the concrete walls demand little attention
you scribble and I am with your thoughts
when the word is orange *naranja taronja*
our spritz, our balcony at sunset 'But I can
never see the star' just luminous white
sheets demand my tension, enters circuits
of setting /// flickering corner spots ///
/// the presences pressing /// the order
of the day is what's left of the day /// we
shouldn't go out to the unconcrete anything
can happen there, multiple droplets
invisible as chance could slip in /// when
and if attention falls the lines grow
a bougainvillea /// when and if tension
falls spots flicker in the corners of our vision

My oldest date, late-born, la peste
Miasmic honeypot, my sticky-fingered ex.
In April comes the heat, caresses
& chocolate mousse, breathily I curse your
boxes of sweaty lingerie left on the doorstep.
You stalk the house, hang outside the school
like a stain on a white sheet, faint but fast.
Baked in, dreamt out, coughed up,
My ancient swan-song, my furtive memory.
The citizens panic and you smirk dispersing,
Sowing wide in arcs, scattering to earth
To hand to mouth, in hospital, the sirens.
You never tire, I remember, liked
To roll in the bedclothes for days
Until I was sore and lost my hope.
You are my old familiar, back now
But I know how this plays out
stay in & wait.

Esperar in Spanish and Catalan means waiting,
means hoping: if I "espero" I wait/I hope and/or
I hope/I wait as I waited and hoped, and/or as
I hoped and waited until time turned into a flickering
thaumatrope / we held our air / we sighed / we
grasped some air in 2, 1 / held it in 2, 1 / we sighed
in 4, 3, 2, 1 / the sirens accompanied the flickering:
ni-no, ni-no, which means neither this nor that,
or not yet at least, at last untickling itself
indoors I hoped I could say something / I waited /
perhaps one day we will look back / I hope still
as I wait

We will look back & we
won't recall: I call it now.
Aspartame fools of the year,
We are shitting shepherds,
every one.
      You too. Sad face with presents wrapped,
      puny desires sore as scabs half-picked.
      Sit on your log as the children beat it
      They will have suffered without words.
There is always the to come, they say.
We will have opened the champagne,
Richest of nations!   Our streets paved
With homelessness & empty vials.
We will not have learned, I can see
glassy-eyed. We will have rejoiced
and not redistributed. We can
procure but not protect. We can
fail magnificently, once again:
our spikey gift
to the futures
market.

We are *caganers* shitting on the pavement,
everyone, fertilising the cracks for the weeds
        that come and go
stuck under some jogger trainers my joy goes
stuck under some jogger's ceiling my joy goes
at the end of the world
              the jogger / cough cough /
              his route / cough cough /
              hydroxychloroquine
              & mince pies
        we won't learn because there's nothing
        to learn because we already knew-know
        everything there is to know and never did
        and still don't (*shush*)

        The bells are tolling in Argentina

    The bells are tolling in Chile

The bells are tolling in Hong Kong (*bong bong*)

& the dreamy computers turn off at once in front of our
glassy-eyes, in front of all the women and men
archetypes muted Zoom participants of this endless
year talks, lost in languages, we are left in silence
knitting that scarf I always wanted to pick up the thread

The tissue I pass around you
Threads I weave into a pouch
To hold you soft against my
stomach
Cocooned in your struggle.
Here you are, mummified
in silken strands
my homemade chrysalis
for a wing beat
of life.
Are you caught or carried,
Crying or cradled,
Between the brittle strands
Of knowing and not knowing,
I hold you tight and listen –
Do you breathe?

COLLABORATION STATEMENT
Jennifer Cooke & Jèssica Pujol Duran

In our initial meeting, we discussed a meme which had circulated on social media at the start of pandemic lockdowns in March-April 2020. The memes came in different versions but the idea was that they converted a normal floorplan of a flat, relabelling different rooms as substitutes for the places one would visit as part of a normal non-lockdown life. For example, the kitchen was relabelled the 'restaurant', the lounge as the 'gym', and the bedroom as 'the office', and so on. We were interested in writing into, out of, and for the spaces of domestic containment that the memes highlighted. Some of the traces of that first conversation are evident in the poems we wrote, the title, and in the visual organisation we imposed upon the finished result. We wrote poems in response to one another, with Jèssica starting first. Each poet picked up upon and responded to the poem that had gone before, so that each poem echoes, extends, stretches and re-inscribes aspects of what preceded it. Much of lockdown was experienced as repetition, captured in this procedure.

Momtaza Mehri
&
A. E. Stallings

Insula

Loose-limbed, we walk the languid length of this island.
Tall reeds brushing bare ankles. Melting into the afternoon's haze,
We tread ribboned dirt. Mimic the regular inching of tidal surrender.
We want to feel this small. To be deliberate with how we use our hands.
So much time, so little we are portioned. Its rise and fall
Crashing against a breaking horizon, a directionless arrow.

Less to do. More to be grateful for. The mouth is a needle-tipped arrow.
From it, regrets tumble like freshwater, echo against our island
Of calcified isolation. Awash with choice, we count the fall
Of last defenses. Watch them dissolve into a slush of doubt and haze.
Days measured by their lonely likeness, their lemon-scented rub of hands.
Inked promises evaporating on flip calendars of surrender.

Is there more to leave behind, to surrender?
Shrug off your armaments of fear, the singed guilt of sling and arrow.
Never this alone, we are a sweep of plans and faltering hands.
The future is cruelly immaculate. Here, is our island
Of unmoored sleeping schedules. Waves of downy-feathered haze
Lift us from grief's oily dread. By the wayside, intentions fall

Purer than than ever. Hook, line, sinker, fall.
Hooked on the news from faraway, where surrender
Is the policy for war with the invisible, while the haze
Of pollution clears from an enameled sky, where no arrow
Of contrail, the chalk-white vector, points away from the island.
The island is also a ship, as a hospital is a ship, with all hands

On deck, below deck? We wait on the (ship's?) bench. A show of hands
For the horizon—no, they are sea-daffodils, unfurling into the fall
Their tattered white sails out of summer, scenting the island
With their perfume of distance, blank semaphores of surrender.
Apollo, the far-shooter, settles his notched, death-fletched arrow
Onto a plangent gut string, and aims with a twang at the haze

Of the horizon. Other islands ride the haze
Like a pod of pirates turned into dolphins. The dawn's hands,
Red from washing the breakfast dishes, arrow
Their finger light into the suds of the tide. Sea mews fall
Into the wake of the last ferry. Does the answer render
The question moot? Silence is the siren of this island.

A haze of white-breasted herons lament above us, their earthly fall
An arrow of descent, of winged surrender.
Hands cradled in laps, our palms a stretch across this thin membrane
      between man and island.

COLLABORATION STATEMENT
Momtaza Mehri & A. E. Stallings

We began with an ongoing exchange in the form of an interview sharing our lockdown and quarantine experiences; what we were reading, how we were writing, or getting through our days, and, as poets, the pandemic's new lexicon (and ancient etymology). At the beginning of quarantine, Alicia was on a Greek island, Momtaza was writing from a Tunisian coastal town; the shared waters of the Mediterranean were a surprising point of contact. Water acts as both boundary and possibility. A sestina seemed like a form that could convey the ambivalent sense of meandering repetition and limitation that quarantine imposed.

Momtaza initiated the repetends and the first stanzas, and Alicia picked up the baton for the last stanzas. The envoi was the result of mutual adjustments and suggestions. We both attempted to contrast the mythical with the mundane, drawing from the etymological roots of pandemic-related words that have seeped into our everyday vocabulary. Each poet made an effort to incorporate words and images from the other poet's "interviews." The speaker could be Circe, an inclusive yet insular first-person plural. The arrows could belong to Apollo, the far shooter.

This poem considers isolation as a kind of insulation from the outside world, derived from the Latin *insulatus* – to make into an island. How do we cross these gulfs to reach each other? How do we extend grace across our respective shores?

CONTRIBUTORS' BIOGRAPHIES

Rachael Allen's first collection of poems is *Kingdomland*, published by Faber. She is the recipient of a Northern Writers Award and an Eric Gregory award. She hosts the Faber Poetry Podcast, is the poetry editor for *Granta* and Granta books, and is currently an Anthony Burgess Fellow at Manchester University.

Anthony Caleshu is the author of four books of poems, most recently, *A Dynamic Exchange Between Us* (Shearsman Books, 2019), and three critical books about poetry, most recently, editor of *In the Air: The Poetry of Peter Gizzi* (Wesleyan University Press, 2018). His latest poems and short fiction can be found in *Manchester Review, Mechanic's Institute Review* and *Granta online*. He is Professor of Poetry and Creative Writing at University of Plymouth, where he leads the MA Creative Writing, and runs the small poetry press, Periplum.

Vahni Capildeo is Writer in Residence at the University of York (2020-22) and Contributing Editor at *PN Review*. Capildeo's recent work incudes *Skin Can Hold* (Carcanet, 2019), *Odyssey Calling* (Sad Press, 2020), and *Light Site* (Periplum, 2020).

Jennifer Cooke is a London-based poet and a Senior Lecturer in English at Loughborough University specialising in contemporary literature and theory. Her poetry can be found online, in print, and in anthologies such as *Out of Everywhere 2: Linguistically Innovative Poetry by Women in the US and the UK*, ed. Emily Critchley (Reality Street, 2015). She is the author of *Apocalypse Dreams* (Sad Press, 2015) and **not suitable for domestic sublimation* (Contraband Books, 2010). Her academic work frequently engages with contemporary poetry, most recently by Andrea Brady, Rob Halpern, Vanessa Place, and Sophie Robinson.

Inua Ellams, born in Nigeria, is a poet, playwright and performer, graphic artist and designer and founder of: *The Midnight Run* (an arts-filled, night-time, urban walking experience), *The Rhythm and Poetry Party* (The R.A.P Party) which celebrates poetry & hip hop, and *Poetry + Film / Hack* (P+F/H) which celebrates Poetry and Film. Identity, displacement and destiny are reoccurring themes in his work, where he tries to mix the old with the new: traditional African oral storytelling with contemporary poetics, paint with pixel, texture with vector. His books are published by Flipped Eye, Akashic, Nine Arches, Penned In The Margins, Oberon & Methuen.

Iain Galbraith is a poet and essayist whose most recent publications include a volume of poems *The True Height of the Ear* (Arc, 2018) as well as translations of Esther Kinsky's prose work *River* (Fitzcarraldo, 2018), Esther Dischereit's *Sometimes a Single Leaf: Selected Poems* (Arc, 2020) and Reinhard Jirgl's novel *The Unfinished* (Seagull, 2020). He has received many prizes for his work, including the Stephen Spender Prize (2014), the Popescu Prize for European Poetry Translation (2015) and the Schlegel-Tieck Prize in 2016 and 2019. Iain was born and grew up in the West of Scotland and lives in Wiesbaden, Germany.

Eleanor Goodman is the award-winning author of the poetry collection *Nine Dragon Island* (2016), and the translator of *Something Crosses My Mind: Selected Poems of Wang Xiaoni* (2014), *Iron Moon: An Anthology of Chinese Workers Poetry* (2017), *The Roots of Wisdom: Poems by Zang Di* (2017), and *Days When I Hide My Corpse in a Cardboard Box: Poems of Natalia Chan* (2018). Her translation of the poetry of Zheng Xiaoqiong is forthcoming in 2021. She is a Research Associate at the Harvard University Fairbank Center.

Stacy Hardy is a writer, an editor at pan-African platform *Chimurenga* and a teacher. Her short fiction is published in journals and literary anthologies around the world and she was the winner of the 2018 Brittle Paper Award for African Fiction and a finalist in the 2018 Caine Prize. Her short fiction collection, *Because the Night*, was published by Pocko (London) in 2015. She regularly collaborates with Angolan composer Victor Gama on multimedia musical works and her experimental one-woman play, *Museum of Lungs* (2018–2019), was performed in South Africa, Egypt and throughout Europe. She is currently working on a research-and-performance-based collaborative endeavour on the geographies and biographies of breath with Chicago-based anthropologist Kaushik Sunder Rajan and South African musician Neo Muyanga, as well as a libretto for a new opera with Lebanese composer Bushra El-Turk and Egyptian director Laila Soliman.

David Herd's collections of poetry include *All Just* (Carcanet, 2012), *Outwith* (Bookthug 2012), *Through* (Carcanet, 2016), *Walk Song* (Equipage, 2018), and *Songs from the Language of a Declaration* (Periplum, 2019). His essays and poems have been widely published in magazines, journals and newspapers and his recent writings on the politics of human movement have appeared in *From the European South*, *Los Angeles Review of Books*, *Paideuma*, and the *Times Literary Supplement*. He is Professor of Modern Literature at the University of Kent and a co-organiser of the project *Refugee Tales*.

Selima Hill lives by the sea in Dorset, England. She is the author of nineteen books of poetry, many of which have been UK Poetry Book Society Choices or Recommendations. Her honours include winning a Whitbread Poetry Award (for *Bunny*, 2001), shortlistings for the Forward Poetry Prize and the Costa

Poetry Award (*People Who Like Meatballs*, 2012), and three shortlisted titles for the T. S. Eliot Prize: *Violet* (1997), *Bunny* (2001), *Jutland* (2015). Her twentieth collection, *Men Who Feed Pigeons*, is forthcoming from Bloodaxe.

Hwang Yu Won was born in Ulsan in 1982. He received a BA in Religious Studies and Philosophy from Sogang University and is currently getting his Ph.D in Indian Philosophy at Dongguk University. His book of poetry *Everything in the World, Maximized* won the Kim Soo-Young prize.

Ilya Kaminsky is the author of *Deaf Republic* (Faber) which was shortlisted for both the T. S. Eliot Prize and the Forward Prize for Best Collection, and won the *Los Angeles Times* Book Award.

Luke Kennard is a poet and novelist who lives in Birmingham. His second collection, *The Harbour Beyond the Movie*, was shortlisted for the Forward Prize in 2007 and his fifth, *Cain*, was shortlisted for the Dylan Thomas Prize 2017. His sixth book of poetry, *Notes on the Sonnets* and his second novel, *The Answer to Everything*, will both be published in 2021.

Carol Leeming MBE FRSA, born in Leicester, England, of Jamaican and Antiguan parents, is a multi-award-winning poet, and a multi-disciplinary artist in literature, performing arts & digital media. Her debut chapbook *The Declamations of Cool Eye,* was well received, selling out its first edition. Her poetry features in numerous poetry anthologies, and her choreopoetry is referenced in *The Cambridge University Companion to British & Asian Literature 1945–2010.* Carol lives in Leicester, and is a Lecturer in Performing Arts at De Montfort University.

Yana Lucila Lema Otavalo is an award-winning video artist, translator, cultural manager, poet and Kichwa Otavalo storyteller from Ecuador. She has recently published a Kichwa-Spanish poetry collection *Tamyawan Shamukupani* (Tujaal Editions, 2018). She teaches in the School of Literature at the Universidad de las Artes del Ecuador.

Jake Levine translated a book of experimental writing by the Lithuanian poet Tomas Butkus' *GOD / THING* (Vario Burnos, 2011), and various works by Kim Yi Deum, Hwang Yu Won and Kim Kyung Ju. The recipient of numerous grants and awards, including a Korean Government scholarship and a Fulbright scholarship, his translations, essays, and writing have appeared in places such as *The New York Times*, *The Literary Review*, etc. Additionally, he writes a series of syndicated articles about contemporary poetry in the Korean literary magazine *Munjang* and the American journal *Entropy*. He is the author of two poetry chapbooks, *The Threshold of Erasure* (Spork Press, 2010) and

Vilna Dybbuk (Country Music, 2014). He has been an editor at Spork Press since 2010 and is currently getting his PhD in comparative literature at Seoul National University. He received his MFA in poetry from the University of Arizona in 2010.

Momtaza Mehri is a poet and independent researcher. Her work has appeared in *Granta*, *Artforum*, the *Guardian*, *BOMB Magazine*, and *Poetry Review*. She is the former Young People's Laureate for London. Her latest pamphlet, *Doing the Most with the Least*, was published by Goldsmiths Press.

Arvind Krishna Mehrotra's recent books include *Translating the Indian Past and Other Literary Histories* (Permanent Black) and *Selected Poems and Translations* (NYRB). Five of the poems from 'Lockdown Garden' previously appeared in *Poetry* magazine.

Sharmistha Mohanty is the author of three works of prose, *Book One, New Life*, and *Five Movements in Praise*. Her most recent work is a book of poems, *The Gods Came Afterwards*. Her work has been published in journals all over the world including *Poetry, Granta, World Literature Today,* and the Chinese journal *Jintian*. A chapbook made from a selection of poems from *The Gods Came Afterwards* appeared early 2020 from Ediciones Pen Presse in Spanish. The poems are translated by the acclaimed Argentinian poet, Mercedes Roffe. Mohanty is the founder-editor of the online literature journal, *Almost Island* and the initiator of the *Almost Island Dialogues*, an annual international writers' gathering held in New Delhi. She has taught for several years at the International Creative Writing MFA program at the City University of Hong Kong.

Sinéad Morrissey is the author of six poetry collections. Her awards include a Lannan Literary Fellowship, first prize in the UK National Poetry Competition, the *Irish Times* Poetry Prize (2009, 2013), and the T. S. Eliot Prize (2013). In 2016 she received the E. M. Forster Award from the American Academy of Arts and Letters. Her most recent collection, *On Balance* (2017), was the winner of the Forward Prize for Best Collection and of the European Poet of Freedom Award. Her first UK selected poems, *Found Architecture*, was published by Carcanet in May 2020. She is Professor of Creative Writing at Newcastle University and the Director of the Newcastle Centre for the Literary Arts.

Omar Musa is a Malaysian-Australian author, poet and rapper from Queanbeyan, New South Wales, Australia. He has released three solo hip hop records and three books of poetry. His debut novel, *Here Come the Dogs*, was published in 2014, and was long-listed for the Miles Franklin Award. Musa was named one of the Young Novelists of the Year by the *Sydney Morning Herald* in 2015.

Togara Muzanenhamo was born in Zambia and brought up in Zimbabwe. He studied Business Administration in the Netherlands and France. He has published three collections of poetry, including *Gumiguru* (Carcanet, 2014), and a fourth is forthcoming from Carcanet in 2021. He lives with his partner and two children in Harare.

André Naffis-Sahely is the author of the collection *The Promised Land: Poems from Itinerant Life* (Penguin, 2017) and the pamphlet *The Other Side of Nowhere* (Rough Trade, 2019), and the editor of *The Heart of a Stranger: An Anthology of Exile Literature* (Pushkin Press, 2020). He is from Abu Dhabi, but was born in Venice to an Iranian father and an Italian mother. His writing has appeared in *The Economist*, *New Statesman*, *Harper's*, *The Nation*, *Poetry*, *The Baffler*, *The Chimurenga Chronic*, *The Believer* and *Playboy*. He has translated over twenty titles of fiction, poetry and nonfiction, including works by Honoré de Balzac, Émile Zola, Abdellatif Laâbi, Alessandro Spina, Frankétienne, Ribka Sibhatu and Tahar Ben Jelloun. He is a Visiting Teaching Fellow at the Manchester Writing School and is the editor of *Poetry London*.

Mariko Nagai was born in Tokyo and raised in Europe and America, and is Professor of Creative Writing and Japanese Literature at Temple University, Japan Campus in Tokyo. Her numerous honours include the Erich Maria Remarque Fellowship from New York University, fellowships from the Rockefeller Foundation Bellagio Center, Akademie Schloss Solitude, UNESCO-Aschberg Bursaries for the Arts, Yaddo, and Writers' Centre of Norwich, to name a few. She has received Pushcart Prizes both in poetry and fiction. Nagai's collection of poems, *Histories of Bodies*, won the Benjamin Saltman Prize from Red Hen Press, and her first collection of stories, *Georgic: Stories* won the 2009 G.S. Sharat Chandra Fiction Prize from BkMk Press. Her other books include *Dust of Eden* (Albert Whitman & Co, 2014), *Irradiated Cities* (Les Figues, 2016), *Under the Broken Sky* (Macmillan, 2019), *Body of Empire* (forthcoming, Tarpaulin Sky Press, 2021) and *The Sword of Yesterday* (forthcoming, Little Brown, 2022).

Vivek Narayanan's books of poems include *Life and Times of Mr S* and the forthcoming *After: A Writing Through Valmiki's Ramayana* (NYRB Poets, 2022).

Alvin Pang is a poet, writer and editor whose broad creative practice spans over two decades of literary activity in Singapore and elsewhere. Featured in the *Oxford Companion to Modern Poetry in English*, his writing has been translated into more than twenty languages, including Swedish, Croatian and Macedonian. His titles include *When the Barbarians Arrive* (Arc, 2012), *What Happened: Poems 1997–2017* (Math Paper Press, 2017) and *Uninterrupted Time* (Recent Work Press, 2019). He completed a PhD in writing in 2020.

Jèssica Pujol Duran (Barcelona, 1982) is a poet, translator and academic, currently working at the Universidad de Santiago de Chile. She writes and translates in Catalan, English and Spanish, and has published chapbooks and books in the three languages. Her more recent publications include *Mare* (Carnaval Press, 2018) and *ninó* (Pont del petroli, 2019). She edits the poetry magazine *Alba Londres,* and is also the editor and translator of a forthcoming anthology of contemporary English poetry in Catalan, *Llengües de foc* (Lleonard Muntaner, 2021), and co-editor of an anthology of Latin American women's poetry, *Temporary Archives: Latin American Women's Poetry* (Arc, 2021).

Vidyan Ravinthiran was born in Leeds, England to Sri Lankan Tamils. He is the author of two books of poetry, the most recent of which, *The Million-Petalled Flower of Being Here*, was a Poetry Book Society Recommendation. He has also written an award-winning study of Elizabeth Bishop. He teaches at Harvard University.

Rakhshan Rizwan has a PhD in Comparative Literature from Utrecht University in the Netherlands. She is the winner of the Judith Khan Memorial Prize for Poetry (2015). Her debut pamphlet, *Paisley* (2017), was shortlisted for the Saboteur Award and the Michael Marks Award. She is the author of *Kashmiri Life Narratives* (2020), a monograph which explores the intersections between human rights and literature in the Valley of Kashmir. She speaks four languages and is originally from Pakistan but has lived in Germany and the Netherlands. She currently lives in the Bay Area in California.

Declan Ryan's debut pamphlet was published in the Faber New Poets series in 2014, and a second pamphlet, *Fighters, Losers*, was published by New Walk Editions in 2019 and was shortlisted for the Michael Marks Award for best pamphlet. He is a regular reviewer of poetry.

Craig Santos Perez is an indigenous Chamoru poet from the Pacific Island of Guam. He is the author of five collections of poetry and the co-editor of five anthologies. He teaches in the English department at the University of Hawai'i, Manoa.

Zoë Skoulding's recent publications include *A Revolutionary Calendar* (Shearsman Books) and *Poetry and Listening: The Noise of Lyric* (Liverpool University Press). She is Professor of Poetry and Creative Writing at Bangor University.

Hazel Smith has published four poetry volumes including, most recently, *Word Migrants* (Giramondo, 2016). She has also published numerous collaborative performance and multimedia works. In 2018, with Will Luers and Roger Dean, she was awarded first place in the Electronic Literature Organisation's Robert

Coover prize. Hazel is Emeritus Professor in the Writing and Society Research Centre, Western Sydney University. She has authored several academic books including *The Contemporary Literature-Music Relationship: intermedia, voice, technology, cross-cultural exchange* (Routledge, 2016). Her website is at www.australysis.com

A. E. Stallings is an American poet who has lived in Greece since 1999. She has published four collections of poetry (most recently *Like*, a finalist for the Pulitzer Prize), and three volumes of verse translation (of Lucretius, Hesiod, and the pseudo-Homeric epic, *The Battle Between the Frogs and the Mice*). She has received fellowships from the Guggenheim and MacArthur Foundations. Her *Selected Poems* is due out from Farrar Straus & Giroux and Carcanet in 2022.

George Szirtes's first book of poems, *The Slant Door* (Secker, 1979) was joint-winner of the Faber Prize. He has published many since then, his collection, *Reel*, winning the T. S. Eliot Prize in 2004, for which he has been twice shortlisted since. His memoir of his mother, *The Photographer at Sixteen* (MacLehose, 2019) won the James Tait Black prize for Biography. His translations from Hungarian poetry and fiction have also won numerous prizes including the Man Booker International for his translations of László Krasznahorkai. He is a Fellow of the Royal Society of Literature.

Harriet Tarlo's single author poetry publications are with Shearsman Books and Etruscan Books and her artists' books with Judith Tucker are with Wild Pansy Press. She is editor of *The Ground Aslant: An Anthology of Radical Landscape Poetry* (Shearsman Books, 2011) and of special features on ecopoetics for *How2* and *Plumwood Mountain*. Her first volume of *Cut Flowers* is out with Guillemot Press in 2021. She is Professor of Ecopoetry and Poetics at Sheffield Hallam University.

Jan Wagner was born 1971 in Hamburg and has been living in Berlin since 1995. Poet, essayist, translator of Anglo-American poetry (Charles Simic, James Tate, Simon Armitage, Jo Shapcott, Sujata Bhatt, Matthew Sweeney, Robin Robertson and others), he has published seven poetry collections since 2001, most recently *Die Live Butterfly Show* (2018). *Regentonnenvariationen* ('Rain Barrel Variations'), his sixth collection, won the Award of the Leipzig Bookfair in 2015; a *Selected Poems 2001–2015* was published by Hanser Verlag. Wagner's poetry has been translated into forty languages. A selection in English (*Self-Portrait With a Swarm of Bees: Selected Poems*, translated by Iain Galbraith) was published in 2015 by Arc; another English selection, translated by David Keplinger, came out in 2017 with Milkweed Editions, under the title *The Art of Topiary: Selected Poems*. Wagner has received various scholarships and awards, among them the Anna Seghers Award (2004), the Friedrich Hölderlin

Award (2011), the Zhongkun International Poetry Prize (China, 2017), the Georg Büchner Prize (2017) and the Prix Max Jacob (France, 2020). He is a member of the German Academy of Language and Literature.

Wang Xiaoni was born in 1955 in Changchun, Jilin Province, China. She graduated from the Jilin University Chinese Department in 1982, and moved to Shenzhen. She has published more than forty books, including collections of essays, short stories, and poetry.

Rory Waterman is the author of three collections with Carcanet: *Tonight the Summer's Over* (2013), a Poetry Book Society Recommendation, shortlisted for a Seamus Heaney Award; *Sarajevo Roses* (2017), shortlisted for the Ledbury Forte Prize, and *Sweet Nothings* (2020). He also publishes a lot of literary criticism. He co-edits New Walk Editions, and is on the English faculty at Nottingham Trent University.

Matthew Welton has published four collections of poetry with Carcanet, including *Squid Squad: A Novel* (2020). Collaboration has been a consistent part of his practice, and he has previously written with the composer Larry Goves, the artist Chris Evans, and the poet Luke Kennard. Matthew teaches creative writing at the University of Nottingham.

Linda Stern Zisquit has published five full-length collections of poetry in the US, most recently *Havoc: New & Selected Poems* and *Return from Elsewhere*. A pamphlet, *From the Notebooks of Korah's Daughter*, was published in the UK by New Walk Editions in 2019. Born in Buffalo, NY, she lives in Jerusalem, Israel, where she writes, translates, teaches and runs a small art gallery.

www.ingramcontent.com/pod-product-compliance
Lightning Source LLC
Chambersburg PA
CBHW030900170426
43193CB00009BA/683